Florence Sandler
<u>1984</u>

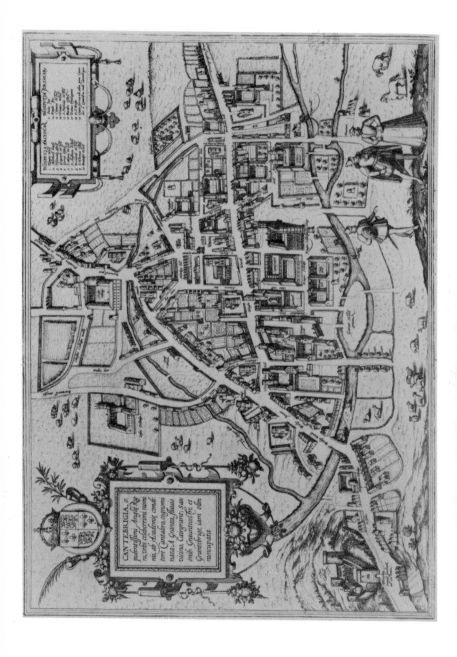

Catholic Cambridge

M.N.L. Couve de Murville
Philip Jenkins

Catholic Truth Society
1983

1 (facing title page). Map of Cambridge, 1575, from Civitates orbis terrarum, *volume ii, published in Cologne by Georg Braun and Frans Hogenberg. It is derived from the first known map of Cambridge drawn by Richard Lyne for J. Caius,* De antiquitate Cantabrigiensis Academiae *(London, 1574). Though fanciful in some of its details, this view from the west clearly reproduces the lay-out of Cambridge soon after the close of the Middle Ages. The King's Ditch is shown circling the town on the east and south. The buildings of the 'Augustine friers' are still standing; part of the buildings of Blackfriars are shown in Preachers Street. The site of Greyfriars is enclosed by walls, with a bridge over the King's Ditch, but the buildings have disappeared.*

The castle is shown (lower left hand corner), guarding the strategic crossing of the river Cam at the Great Bridge (now Magdalene Bridge). The convergence of the roads on the right bank at a point some two hundred yards from the bridge indicates that at the time when these tracks came into being, before the existence of a town, the land by the river was marshy and unapproachable. The present-day Bridge Street may rest on an artificial causeway.

Tantae molis erat Romanam condere gentem
Virgil, *Aeneid,* I, 33.

TO
THE CANONESSES OF ST AUGUSTINE
AT
LADY MARGARET HOUSE
WHO
PROVIDED THE HAVEN
WHERE
THIS BOOK COULD BE COMPLETED

First published 1983 by the
Incorporated Catholic Truth Society
38–40 Eccleston Square
London SW1V 1PD

Nihil Obstat: Mgr H. Francis Davis, Censor
Imprimatur: Mgr Ralph Brown, V.G.
Westminster, 1983

ISBN 0 85183 494 9

Acknowledgement and thanks for permission to reproduce the photographs are due to the Syndics of Cambridge University Library for plates 1, 5, 6 and 7; to the Committee for Aerial Photography for plates 2 and 12; to the Committee of Management of the University Combination Room for plate 10; to the President and Fellows of Queens' College for plate 13; to the Master and Fellows of St John's College for plate 16; to the parish priest of Our Lady and the English Martyrs for plates 18, 19, 20 and 21; and to C.U.C.A. for plates 22, 23, 24 and 25. Plates 3 and 4 are copyright by Brother C. Pearson, S.S.F.; we are grateful to the Master and Fellows of Corpus Christi College for allowing these photographs to be taken and also for the photograph reproduced on plate 8. The Provost and Fellows of King's College have allowed us to reproduce the photographs on plate 5 and the coloured photograph on the front cover.

Printed and bound in England by
Staples Printers Rochester Limited
at the Stanhope Press

Contents

Abbreviations viii
Preface ix

1. The Town before the University   1
2. The University in the Middle Ages 13
   The Studies in Medieval Cambridge 19
   The Friars in Cambridge 23
      The Franciscans or Greyfriars 23
      The Dominicans or Blackfriars 26
      The Carmelites or Whitefriars 28
      The Austin Friars 30
   The First Colleges 34
   The University in the Late Middle Ages 41
3. St John Fisher and the Catholic Reform 55
4. Cambridge and the Reformation 68
5. Sawston Hall and Survival in Penal Times 90
6. The Nineteenth Century Revival of Catholicism 98
7. Consolidation in Town and University 113
   The Parishes 113
   The University Chaplaincy 120
Appendix I   *Provisional list of members of the*
              University of Cambridge who were executed
              or who died in prison for the Catholic Faith
              during the period of the Reformation. 139
Appendix II   *Missionary Rectors and Parish Priests of*
              Our Lady and the English Martyrs
              Cambridge. 144
Appendix III *Catholic Chaplains at the University of*
              Cambridge. 144
Index 145

Abbreviations

AAW	Archives of the Archbishop of Westminster, London.
Anstruther	Godfrey Anstruther, O.P., *The Seminary Priests,* 4 volumes, (Ware, Durham and Great Wakering, 1969–77).
BL	British Library.
BRUC	A. B. Emden, *A Biographical Register of the University of Cambridge to 1500* (Cambridge, 1963).
BRUO	A. B. Emden, *A Biographical Register of the University of Oxford A.D. 1501 to 1540* (Oxford, 1974).
CambRO	Cambridgeshire Record Office.
Camm, *N.M.Monks*	B. Camm, O.S.B., *Nine Martyr Monks* (London, 1931).
CASPubl	Cambridge Antiquarian Society Publications.
Challoner	R. Challoner, *Memoirs of Missionary Priests,* new edition (London, 1924).
Cooper	C. H. Cooper and T. Cooper, *Athenae Cantabrigienses,* 3 volumes (1858–1913).
CPR	*Calendar of Entries in the Papal Registers relating to Great Britain and Ireland* (London 1893–).
CRS	Catholic Record Society publications.
DNB	*Dictionary of National Biography.*
HE	Bede, *Historia Ecclesiastica Gentis Anglorum.*
LEM	B. Camm, O.S.B., ed., *Lives of the English Martyrs,* first series, two volumes (London, 1904–5).
LP	*Calendar of Letters and Papers of the Reign of Henry VIII,* edited by J. S. Brewer, etc., 21 volumes (London, 1864–1932).
ROE	D. Knowles, *The Religious Orders in England,* 3 volumes (Cambridge, 1956–9).
RS	Rolls Series.
ULC	University Library Cambridge.
Van Ortroy	François Van Ortroy, S.J., ed., *Vie du bienheureux martyr Jean Fisher* (Brussels, 1893).
VCH	Victoria County History, Cambridgeshire volumes.
Venn, *Al.Can.*	John Venn and J. A. Venn, *Alumni Cantabrigienses,* Part I (earliest times to 1751), 4 volumes (Cambridge, 1922–7); Part II (from 1752 to 1900), 6 volumes (Cambridge, 1940–54).
Venn, *Gonv. and Caius*	John Venn, *Biographical History of Gonville and Caius College 1349–1897,* 4 volumes (Cambridge, 1897–1912).

Preface

Catholic Cambridge was the title of a pamphlet by Fr G. J. MacGillivray, published by the CTS in 1933. As it has long been out of print, the idea occurred to us independently of writing a new study of the subject and we were delighted to be put in touch by the CTS and to collaborate on the project. Philip Jenkins wrote chapters 1, 3, 4, 5 and 6; Maurice Couve de Murville wrote chapters 2 and 7 and prepared the manuscript for publication. We both had to work in a hurry and with the pressure of other commitments as Philip Jenkins left Cambridge in 1980 to become Assistant Professor of the History of Justice at Pennsylvania State University and Maurice Couve de Murville left in 1982 to become Archbishop of Birmingham.

Although our study has wider limits than that of G. J. MacGillivray and has included the Catholic Church in the town as well as in the university, we have retained the title of his booklet; there is a certain piquancy in bringing together words with such contrasting associations. Cambridge is usually thought of as the home of the English Reformation, the university of Latimer, Ridley, Cranmer and Matthew Parker, set in the eastern counties of Oliver Cromwell and John Bunyan. The evangelical revival initiated in late eighteenth-century Cambridge by Charles Simeon is readily contrasted with the catholicising movement to which Oxford has given its name. We have tried to show that the Catholic beliefs which permeated a complex society in the Middle Ages have had a remarkable story of survival and that, in recent times, they have continued to inspire new generations and to preside at the setting up of new institutions.

However we would like to disclaim any exclusiveness which the title of our book could appear to revive; we are well aware that *Catholic Cambridge* is now one Cambridge among many others and that, since the Second Vatican Council, the Catholic Church has proclaimed its intention of encouraging all that is good in other traditions while maintaining the unique character of its own proclamation of the truth. It seeks to serve, not to dominate, but the claims of the truth are best served by an understanding of the sufferings and disappointments, as well as the joys and achievements, of a long past. If we have that understanding, we shall not underestimate the challenge of a true rapprochement between the Christians of today.

We would like to express our thanks for the great help we have received from Mrs Dorothy Owen, Keeper of the University Archives, who willingly put her erudition and her time at our disposal. Mr J. C. T. Oates, Fellow of Darwin College, kindly allowed us to consult his history of the University Library in typescript; we have also been helped by Dr E. S. Leedham-Green, the Assistant Keeper of the Archives, and by Mr R. H. Fairclough of the Map Room in the University Library. Mr P. C. Barry, Research Assistant for the Cause of the English and Welsh Martyrs at Farm Street, provided the list of Cambridge martyrs, reproduced as Appendix I, for which we are grateful. On particular points we have had patient help from Dr Oliver Rackham, Fellow of Corpus Christi College; Miss Rosemary Graham of Trinity College Library; Mr A. Nicholls, Librarian of the University Library, Birmingham and Dr P. F. Hammond, Lecturer at the University of Leeds. We have learnt a lot from conversations on various aspects of our subject with Fr Osmund Lowry, O.P.; Dr Eamonn Duffy, Fellow of Magdalene College; Dr John Morrill, Fellow of Selwyn College and Dr Dominic Bellenger of Downside School.

The following have read our manuscript, in whole or in part, and have made many valuable suggestions: Dr Elizabeth Stopp, Fellow of Girton; Dom Adrian Morey, Master of Benet House; Fr Michael Hackett of Austin Friars, Carlisle; Fr Robert Ombres of Blackfriars, Cambridge, and Dr Simon Keynes, Fellow of Trinity College. For the errors and shortcomings which remain we are, of course, entirely responsible.

We are grateful to the Bishop of Ely for allowing us to quote from the archives of the diocese, deposited in the University Library, and to the President and Fellows of Queens' College for permission to quote from their archives which are also at the

University Library, Cambridge. Major A. C. Eyre has allowed us to quote from the Huddleston papers, deposited at the Cambridgeshire Record Office. We wish to acknowledge the permission from Dr K. J. Egan and Dr R. H. Pogson to quote from their unpublished doctoral dissertations of the University of Cambridge. The editors of the *Fisher House Newsletter* and of *Forum* have allowed us to reproduce material first published by them. We have acknowledged individually the sources of the photographs reproduced but we would like to thank here Mr Andrew Gough of Trinity College and Mr Alan Rooke of St John's College who took many photographs of Cambridge especially for this book. Our thanks too to Mrs Hazel Hedge for dealing so well with the complications of a serialised typescript.

We are very conscious of the limitations of this book. It is an impressionist sketch of a vast subject; we nevertheless release it to an indifferent public on Chesterton's principle that a thing worth doing is worth doing badly. Perhaps it may inspire, stimulate or infuriate someone sufficiently to prompt the production of something better.

M. N. L. Couve de Murville
Philip Jenkins

2 (overleaf). Aerial photograph of Cambridge, taken 10 June 1981. Although suburbs have grown to the east and south, the open spaces along the curve of the river enclose the old town of Cambridge in much the same limits as in the sixteenth century. King's College Chapel dominates the middle right foreground (as it does in the sixteenth century view). College buildings have begun to encroach the left bank of the Cam, St John's College's New Court and Cripps Court on the left foreground; Queens' College's Cripps Court on the right foreground (partly out of the picture). The older courts of Trinity, Caius, Trinity Hall and Clare form a regular pattern in the lower centre of the picture.

one:

The Town before the University

An account of Catholic Cambridge should begin with the exam-
ination of the town that stood on the banks of the Granta long
before there was such a thing as a university in Western Europe,
a town which continued to exist and flourish while the university
grew to pre-eminence.[1] It is good to be reminded that the name
of Cambridge has not always been synonymous with higher
education and that this distinction should still be made today.
The town of Cambridge moreover provides an excellent example
of the way in which ecclesiastical and particularly monastic life
dominated a major medieval town. Even if we were only looking
for Catholic Cambridge in medieval survivals – and we will
attempt to do much more than this – it would be evident that the
town has almost as much to offer as the more celebrated university.

The town of Cambridge originated in Roman times around the
area now known as Castle Hill and Mount Pleasant, where streets
like Pound Hill and Pleasant Row long preserved the characteristically straight lines of the Roman fortress. There is a strong
probability that Cambridge is to be identified with the place
called, in the Antonine Itinerary, *Durolipons*[2] and this would
indicate that there was a bridge at this period at the place where
the river could be approached on relatively dry ground and where
it could easily be forded.

Early Cambridge must have had a Christian presence; recent
archaeology has emphasised the extent to which the new religion
permeated the ordinary people of Britain, as is shown, for example,
by finds in the fourth century cemeteries of Cirencester (Glou-

1

cestershire) or Poundbury (Dorset). There is no reason for thinking that Cambridge was any different. By the late fourth century there would probably have been a bishop for every *civitas*, so that the Christians at Cambridge would have been linked to a bishop at Verulamium (St Alban's), or perhaps *Venta Icenorum* (Caistor by Norwich). There must have been a church, probably with its vessels of silver and gold, like those found in 1975 at *Durobrivae* (Water Newton, near Peterborough). However the principal material relics of this early Christianity are not visually exciting, comprising as they do lead baptismal tanks, marked with a *chi-rho* or other Christian symbols. Even by the standards of the Dark Ages we are singularly badly informed about the transition in this area from Roman Britain to Anglo-Saxon England. We can infer that when the first Germanic settlers arrived there was a Roman framework still in existence, since they settled in suburbs outside the Roman areas of settlement. Their burials are pagan but they must have seen the churches in operation until some unspecified date, perhaps in the sixth century. All is uncertain at this period; when we next have evidence of Christianity in the area it is very different. It is new, missionary and Germanic.

The people living between the Cam and the Ouse after the Anglo-Saxon settlements were Middle Angles and they were brought to Christianity by their ruler Peada, son of Penda, king of Mercia, in the middle of the seventh century. According to Bede the first two bishops of this people were Irishmen, Diuma and Ceollach.[3] There was also a Christian influence coming from St Felix's establishment of the church of the East Angles; his successor in the bishopric came from the area of the Gyrwe, that is, roughly, the Cambridgeshire fens.[4] We can infer that the area was converted by mixed influences, Irish from Northumbria and Gallic from East Anglia.

Soon we have evidence that this new Christianity had taken deep roots. Botolph established a monastery at *Icanho*, a deserted spot somewhere in East Anglia, in 654; the excavations carried out at St Botolph's church, Hadstock, in 1974 have provided strong circumstantial evidence for identifying this spot, some twelve miles south east of Cambridge, with *Icanho* and for locating St Botolph's first place of burial under the south transept of the present church.[5] Ely's monastic history dates from 673 when St Etheldreda founded a double monastery there. The site was ideal as a *desert*, in the sense of a place affording complete isolation. Etheldreda, an East Anglian princess, had obtained it through her first marriage to an alderman of the South Gyrwe, the fen people. She died in 679 after a life of great holiness and in 695 her sister decided to place her bones in a stone coffin so that they might be translated into the church. Ely had no suitable stone and the monks therefore sailed to a 'small abandoned city which is called in the language of the English Grantacaestir'.[6] Here they found a white marble sarcophagus of outstanding workmanship with a close-fitting lid and this was used to bury the still uncorrupted body of the saint. Similar sarcophagi have been found in the Roman cemeteries near Cambridge[7] but the interesting thing about this text is that it gives us the earliest Anglo-Saxon name for Cambridge, 'the *castrum* on the Granta'. The absence of any reference to the bridge implies that the Roman bridge had disappeared. It is the same in the life of Guthlac, written by Bede's contemporary, Felix, between 730 and 740. He can only refer to Cambridge as 'the camp which they call by the name of Gronte'.[8] In the next century the annal for 875 in the Anglo-Saxon Chronicle, which was written soon after that date, calls the town *Grante brycge,* the Bridge on the Granta,[9] indicating that by that time the bridge had been rebuilt and Cambridge had been given the name which is at the origin of its modern form. It is thought that Offa, king of Mercia (757–796), who was in control of East Anglia, is likely to have been the builder of the bridge.

Although the origins of medieval Cambridge are obscure, it is possible to form some picture of the social and religious context. The town was of dual origin, with the old Roman centre to the north balanced by a newer one around Market Hill. It must have been a place of importance on the lines of communication between the Midlands and East Anglia; however there is little definite information about its history until 875, when a large Viking army occupied the town for a year. In the wars of reconquest in the next century Cambridge acquired new fortifications, a *burh* and possibly the King's Ditch, which was to mark until the nineteenth century the eastern and southern limits of the town as decisively

3

as the Granta defended the north and the west. Cambridge was for several centuries a garrison town since a vital river crossing had to be defended and royal control maintained over the remote and turbulent area of the fens. The Danes also made their contribution; the trading importance of the town is indicated by the mint which was already in existence in the tenth century, while Danish settlement is suggested by the fact that in the eleventh century the town was divided into ten wards, each under a *lawman,* a Scandinavian name for a Scandinavian structure.

In 1010 the town was burnt down by the Danes but by the time of the Norman Conquest it had about four hundred messuages (i.e. houses and shops) from which we can infer a population of about 2,000, a third of which lived north of the river. There were already ten churches, some of which cannot now be located with certainty, although St Benet's was obviously an important structure, presumably of the eleventh century. The tower of this church is the oldest building in Cambridge, a reminder of the importance of the town before the university. Dedications and surviving architectural fragments suggest pre-Conquest origins for St Botolph's, St Clement's, St Edward's and Little St Mary's. As yet the town had no religious communities but the surrounding area was dominated by a few immensely wealthy monasteries which had been re-endowed with great estates in the late tenth century; among the more famous were Ramsey, Ely, Thorney, Crowland and Peterborough, but there were also a number of smaller houses such as Chatteris.

After 1066 all the trends which we have seen at work in Anglo-Saxon England grew in importance. The fens were the scene of a rebellion against Norman rule and continued to be a possible source of opposition to royal authority, and so Cambridge castle was built on the orders of William the Conqueror in 1068. A bishopric was established in 1109 at Ely which had until then been subject to Lincoln. In 1131 the town obtained a monopoly of the county's waterborne trade; it therefore controlled to some extent the wealth of a fertile area and grew rapidly in prosperity. This was a time of unprecedented expansion of population and consequent demand for food, both in England and in Europe. Until the thirteenth century Cambridge was a port accessible to sea-going ships and it exported food as far afield as Norway from its quays or *hythes*; the hythes were named after their chief item of trade, corn, salt, flax, etc. As well as this seaborne trade, great fairs attracted merchants to Cambridge, Stourbridge Fair from the twelfth century, Garlic and Midsummer Fairs by the thirteenth century. By the later period, there was a Jewish community in the town, always a sign of economic vigour in the Middle Ages. The Jews may have arrived as early as 1101 and they occupied a *Jewry,* first of all in the area around the present Guildhall, later around the present Round Church and All Saints' Passage. All Saints' Church, which stood opposite Trinity College and which was pulled down in the nineteenth century, was commonly called 'All Saints' in Jewry'.

The town of Cambridge enjoyed great importance as an economic and political centre, especially during times of crisis. It was a firm base for royal authority during periodic rebellions in the fens in the mid-twelfth century when, as the saying went, 'Christ and his saints slept.'[10] It was perhaps for the same reason that King John favoured the town, granting it a charter in 1201 and ordering the refurbishing of the King's Ditch in 1215. Cardinal Guala, the papal legate, helped to avert civil war between the king and the barons in 1216, as a result of which Henry III gave him the living of Chesterton; this explains the curious Italian links of that parish over the next two centuries. There was fighting again in the second half of the thirteenth century, as a result of which Edward I decided on his accession in 1272 to rebuild and extend the fortifications of the castle.

This is the context in which we must examine the impressive growth of the religious life of the town. In the first decade of Norman rule, new churches were built, All Saints' by the Castle, St Peter's, Holy Trinity and All Saints' in Jewry. The economic expansion of the late eleventh century coincided with an upsurge in the popularity of monasticism and the appearance of new orders, like the Augustinian canons and the Gilbertine canons. Cambridge after the Conquest was dominated by the Sheriff Picot, whose wife Hugoline was said to have been miraculously cured. In gratitude Picot and Hugoline established a community of six Augustinian canons next to the castle and near the present church of St Giles, where a splendid Norman arch survives in the Victorian fabric. In 1112 the community moved to Barnwell where there grew up around the priory something like a third centre for the town, a pendant to the earlier centres on Castle Hill and Market Hill. Between 1133 and 1138 a house of Benedictine nuns dedicated to St Radegund was founded; its buildings form the nucleus of the present Jesus College. In 1140 the abbot of Ramsey permitted the Fraternity of the Holy Sepulchre to build the Round Church, so that Cambridge can be seen as reflecting the religious trends of the age towards new monastic orders and an interest in the Holy Places fostered by the Crusades. New foundations continued; at the end of the twelfth century a Hospital of St John was founded in the town on a site occupied today by St John's College; the community was composed of a Master and brethren whose task was to care for the sick.

During the thirteenth century the friars contributed six new foundations to Cambridge. Two of them, the Friars of the Sack and the Pied Friars, were short-lived but the other four prospered until the Reformation and are described more fully in the next chapter, where we treat the life of the university. Their fine churches and conventual buildings ringed the centre of the town, so that religious buildings must have dominated its aspect. Apart from the main structures, there were ancillary buildings like the twelfth century leper chapel on the present Newmarket Road and the gatehouse chapel of Barnwell Priory which became the parish church of St Andrew the Less.

Monastic life also impinged on the town in other ways because the fenland abbeys were such great landowners in south Cambridgeshire. In 1319, for instance, a list of services and rents due to Ely notes that a certain Baldwin and his colleagues are to bring supplies to Cambridge from which grain can be sailed to Ely;[11] once again the town appears as a junction for the waterborne trade of the whole region, much of it under the auspices of the monks of Ely.

Religion influenced life in other ways. The merchants and businessmen who dominated the town were united in a prestigious Guild of Saint Mary, with a complex structure reminiscent of a minor religious order. The leading town figures belonged to it

3 (above). Corpus Christi Drinking Horn. This drinking horn was given to the town guild of Corpus Christi by John de Goldcorne, Alderman of the Guild, and was used by the brethren at the feast which followed the Corpus Christi procession. It passed into the possession of Corpus Christi College, founded by the Guild in 1352, and is still used at college feasts; every Fellow and nearly every undergraduate of Corpus Christi has drunk from it. The horn is that of an European auroch and it was probably mounted as a drinking horn in Germany. The silver gilt middle band and the finial date from the fourteenth century and there was origi- nally a cover which has disappeared. The lip band was added c. 1500; the legs and the plaque with the arms of the college date from the seventeenth century. (Photograph by Br. C. Pearson, S.S.F.)

7

from its foundation about 1280. In 1352 it was allowed to coalesce with the Guild of Corpus Christi for the purpose of founding Corpus Christi College; there is evidence from elsewhere of guilds taking part in the endowment of grammar schools but the foundation of a college was a more ambitious undertaking and is unique. The college benefited from its origins in being established right in the centre of the old town, next to the parish church of St Benet which it used for worship before it had its own chapel; it was associated with the guild in the annual procession of the Blessed Sacrament through the streets of Cambridge (see below, page 44) and it also inherited some of the plate of the guild, including the magnificent drinking horn which is still used at college feasts (see plates 3 and 4).

The statutes of the Guild of the Annunciation for 1379 have survived and they show that the guilds served both devotional and charitable aims. This guild met in Great St Mary's church and collected funds from its members which were kept in a common chest. From these a candle was provided which was placed in front of the statue of the Blessed Virgin Mary in the Lady chapel; the candle was lit on the five feasts of Our Lady[12] at matins, prime and second vespers and during high mass, also at high mass on Sundays and every day during the singing of the antiphon of Our Lady. Any brother or sister reduced to poverty was to receive seven pence a week from the common chest as long as there was any money in it.[13]

A good example of the attitude of the wealthy burgesses of Cambridge is provided by Henry Eustace, alderman and first mayor of the town in the early thirteenth century, who gave the

4 (opposite). Corpus Christi Drinking Horn; detail. The finial shows the head of a pope with the papal tiara in its early form. This is probably an allusion to the legend of St Cornelius who is supposed to have received from a griffin whom he had cured a claw which he made into a drinking vessel. There was a pilgrimage to the relics of St Cornelius at Cornelimünster near Aachen and in German medieval art St Cornelius is always shown carrying a horn. This representation of St Cornelius points to a German origin for the Corpus Christi horn. (Photograph by Br. C. Pearson, S.S.F.)

advowson of St Clement's church to St Radegund's Priory and patronised the church's guilds and chantries.

The wills of townsmen right up to the Henrician Reformation are fervent in making bequests for the setting up of altars in particular churches, the maintenance of lights before shrines and the singing of masses by chantry priests, often over a period of several years. Cambridge did not have a nationally celebrated shrine but there was considerable local devotion to the statue of Our Lady in the church of the Dominicans.

In the years 1278–9 an assessment of properties in Cambridge allows us to estimate that the population numbered approximately 3,000, but it had already passed its peak. The economic boom was slackening and discontent is suggested by the growing hostility to the Jews, always an obvious scapegoat. There were appalling anti-Semitic riots in 1266; from 1274 the wearing of the yellow star became compulsory and in 1290 the Jews were expelled from England by Edward I.

The next century was worse. Arable land in the surrounding parishes was going out of cultivation at an alarming rate between 1300 and 1340 because of a sharp decrease in the population; then the Black Death struck in 1348–50, carrying off between fifty and seventy-five per cent of the population. Cambridge endured a recurrence of the plague in 1389–90 and the town suffered major fires in 1290 and 1385. The presence and growing privileges of the secular clerks of the university led to much discontent which was reflected in riots in 1260, 1304 and 1322. In 1381 men from the town and from the surrounding countryside attacked the masters and scholars. There was a regular *jacquerie* in Cambridge; houses of unpopular citizens were sacked; the mayor was forced to lead a band of over a thousand men against Barnwell priory; Corpus Christi College was raided and its muniments burnt. On a Sunday morning the rioters broke into Great St Mary's during mass and broke open the university chest, which was kept in the tower, destroying its documents. Jewels and vessels were seized and a second university chest at the house of the Carmelites was also broken open. The masters and scholars were then compelled by the mayor and bailiffs to renounce all the privileges granted to the university by the kings of England and

10

the charters which recorded them were burnt in the market place. One account tells of an old woman who tossed the ashes of the parchments to the wind chanting, 'Away with the learning of the clerks, away with it.' Order was only restored when the Bishop of Norwich arrived with a band of armed men, but relations between the university and the town were embittered for a long time to come. In 1422 the mayor was again accused of leading an assault on the scholars. The anti-clerical tradition apparently survived in Lollardy, of which there are traces in the mid-fifteenth century in Cambridge, Chesterton and Swaffham. Economic hardship and resentment of the university's growing strength led to a suspicion of the clergy as such; it must be admitted that the town did suffer. Before the fifteenth century one of its main arteries had been Milne Street running down to the river near the present Anchor Inn, where stood the king's mill and the bishop's mill. It was an important street on which stood colleges like Queens', St Catharine's, God's House, Clare and Trinity Hall. But the building of King's College Chapel from 1446 and later the building of Trinity College cut across the old street, leaving only truncated sections. One would also like to know what the townsfolk thought of the suppression of St John's Hospital in 1511 to provide another college for the university. It is often stated that the original foundation was decayed but that is a university point of view, rehearsed to obtain a dissolution of the hospital from the pope. Certainly disputes between the town and the university were still rife under Henry VII when a treaty between the two had to be drawn up by St John Fisher and a board of arbitrators instituted (1503); these troubles were followed almost immediately by another outbreak of the plague.

It is however possible to exaggerate the late medieval decline of Cambridge. In 1388 Richard II held a parliament here and in 1544 the town is described as 'wele inhabyted and replenysshed with people'.[14] Above all, the coming of the university had completely changed the nature and significance of Cambridge which, from being a provincial town, had become one of the centres of European Christendom.

Notes and References to Chapter 1

1. Throughout we have used the volumes of the *Royal Commission for Historical Monuments* on the city of Cambridge; the *Victoria County History* and the *Dictionary of National Biography*. Other works of general use have been C. W. Stubbs, *Story of Cambridge* (London, 1922); Alison Taylor, *Anglo-Saxon Cambridgeshire,* and H. C. Darby, *Medieval Cambridgeshire* (both Oleander Press, Cambridge, 1978 and 1977 respectively) and P. V. Addyman and Martin Biddle, 'Medieval Cambridge', *Proceedings of the Cambridge Archaeological Society,* 58 (1965), pp. 74–137.

2. See *The City of Cambridge,* Royal Commission on Historical Monuments, 1959, i, pp. lxv–lxvi.

3. Bede, *HE* iii, 21; Bertram Colgrave and R. A. B. Mynors, ed., *Bede's Ecclesiastical History of the English People* (Oxford, 1969), pp. 278–80.

4. Bede, *HE* iii, 20 (ed. Colgrave and Mynors, pp. 276–8).

5. See Warwick Rodwell, 'The Archaeological Investigation of Hadstock Church, Essex; an Interim Report', *The Antiquaries Journal* 56 (1976), pp. 51–71.

6. *'venerunt ad civitatulam quandam desolatam . . . quae lingua Anglorum Grantacaestir vocatur', HE* iv, 19 (ed. Colgrave and Mynors, p. 394).

7. See illustrations on Plate I, *The City of Cambridge,* Royal Commission on Historical Monuments, i.

8. *Castellum 'quem dicunt nomine Gronte',* B. Colgrave, *Felix's Life of Guthlac,* (Cambridge, 1956), p. 86.

9. C. Plummer, *Two of the Saxon Chronicles,* (Oxford, 1892), p. 74.

10. Anglo-Saxon Chronicle 1137; Dorothy Whitelock ed., *The Anglo-Saxon Chronicle* (London, 1961), p. 200.

11. S. J. A. Evans, *The Medieval Estate of the Cathedral Priory of Ely,* (Ely, 1973), pp. 11–12.

12. These would probably be the Purification (2 February); the Annunciation (25 March); the Assumption (15 August); the Nativity of Mary (8 September) and the Immaculate Conception (8 December).

13. M. Bateson, *Cambridge Gild Records* (CAS Publ, 1903), pp. 64 & 66.

14. From the Cambridge Paving Act of 1544, quoted in VCH, iii, pp. 13–14.

two:

The University
in the Middle Ages

In the Dark Ages the survival of learning in the western world
had depended to a large extent on monasteries and monastic
schools. Later it was the cathedral schools which produced outstanding teachers and attracted scholars from afar. The emergence
of universities in the twelfth and thirteenth centuries marked a
third stage, in which teachers and students organized themselves
into independent corporations for the sake of study; it is to this
third stage that the origins of the University of Cambridge belong.[1]

The first clear mention of scholars at Cambridge dates from
1209. In that year there was an affray at Oxford and two or three
students were accused of murdering a townswoman; according to
the chronicles, the mayor clapped them into gaol and got in touch
with the king to find out what he should do. At that time King
John was having a major row with the Church; he was probably
glad of an opportunity to string up a few miserable clerics *pour
encourager les autres*. The students were hanged. If it was a
calculated move, it misfired completely. A sore nerve had been
touched, that of ecclesiastical immunity from secular courts; it
was the issue on which St Thomas Becket had staked his life a
generation previously. As members of an ecclesiastical body (see
below, p. 16) students were entitled to judgment in Church courts
and this they had been denied. In protest the whole university of
Oxford, masters and students, left the city. The event is mentioned
by several chronicles[2] but only two of them tell us where they
went. Roger of Wendover says that three thousand scholars left
Oxford and went to Cambridge and Reading.[3] There is no way

13

of checking his figures; strangely, this reference, which is the first certain evidence of the presence of students in Cambridge, is also practically the first clear statement about the existence of a large body of masters and students at Oxford. It can be assumed that they had been there for some time, perhaps from the end of the twelfth century, but nothing certain is known about the origins of the University of Oxford. This has not prevented an Oxford historian from wondering why, after the disturbance of 1209, students and masters from Oxford should have gone to 'that distant marsh town'.[4] One possible reason has been indicated in the previous chapter: Cambridge was a thriving town with plenty of coming and going, and plenty of lodgings. It was also a town free of immediate control from a great magnate, lay or ecclesiastical. These advantages had been present at Oxford, and they were found too in Stamford and Northampton, both of them towns that attracted temporary settlements of scholars and masters at this period.

Another possible reason has been indicated by Fr Michael Hackett, the editor of the earliest known text of the university's statutes; he points out that several of the witnesses who attested the charters of the bishops of Ely at this period are called *magistri*, that is, graduates. One of them, John Grim, a Master of Theology, was master or rector of the schools at Oxford in 1201 and he was still resident there in 1206–9. The Grims were a well known Cambridge family; one of them, the clerk Edward Grim, was present when Archbishop Thomas Becket was murdered in Canterbury Cathedral in 1170 and was wounded when he tried to save the archbishop; other Cambridge names which occur are Blund and Malketon. Should there have been a group of Oxford graduates who had connections both with Cambridge and with the household and administration of the bishops of Ely, they may have persuaded their fellow-masters at Oxford to settle at Cambridge while their own schools at Oxford were closed; by their influence in the town of Cambridge they would have been well placed to make the transition easier.[5] This is a hypothesis, but it would also help to explain the friendly relations which existed from the beginning between the group of scholars at Cambridge and the bishops of Ely.

5. *University Seals. Impression of the seal of the university (left)
in use from c. 1410 to 1580. The legend reads SIGILLVM VNI-
VERSITATIS CANTEBRIGGIE. The chancellor is shown
seated between two scholars; he wears a gown, furred tippet and
round cap and holds a book. The two scholars wear sleeveless
gowns and hoods. Underneath is a bridge spanning a river with
two fishes in it.*

*Impression of the seal of the chancellor (right); the seal dates
from the early thirteenth century and must be contemporary with
the emergence of the office, first mentioned in 1225. The legend
(broken in this example) reads S[IGILLVM] CANCELLARII
VNIVERSITATIS CANTEBRIGIE. The head of the chancellor
is shown in profile, wearing the round cap; underneath is the
bridge and the river with two fishes. The presence on both
university seals of the bridge which gave to Cambridge its name
emphasises the importance of this construction in the life of the
town.* (Archives: King's College)

15

In 1214 the papal legate in England, Nicholas, published an ordinance enjoining penance on the burgesses of Oxford and allowing the masters and scholars to return and resume their lectures. The majority no doubt went back but not all, as is evident from the continuity of the schools at Cambridge after 1214. In 1225 the existence of a chancellor at Cambridge is mentioned for the first time. This is only nine years after the first mention of a chancellor at Oxford and it indicates that the masters and scholars of Cambridge were treated by the bishop of Ely as a distinct corporate body within the diocese, directly under his authority and exempt from the jurisdiction of the archdeacon of Ely and the dean of Cambridge.

Universities in the early Middle Ages were well adapted to migration because they did not own property; masters and students lived in rented lodgings and the teaching was done in rented premises as well. The provision of accommodation was thus of great importance. In 1231 a writ of Henry III provided for the assessment of rents of houses where students lodged in Cambridge. This was to be done by two Masters of Arts and by two townsmen.[6] Another privilege which was granted by the crown to the university was that of fixing the prices of bread, wine and other staple commodities necessary for the sustenance of its members. From this derives the later privilege of the vice-chancellor in licensing premises in Cambridge, of which some aspects survive to this day. The majority of scholars were poor and without some guarantee of this sort against the inflation of prices the university could not have survived. In a way, these privileges were the equivalent of the grants which a modern government makes to students and to universities.

The strangest aspect of a medieval university from our point of view was its ecclesiastical character. As an academic corporation the university was an ecclesiastical body. Once elected, the chancellor was confirmed by the bishop of Ely and derived from him his jurisdiction, so that he had the same powers as the archdeacon of the diocese, and indeed more. He had ordinary jurisdiction over all members of the university and also in cases involving a member of the university and a member of the general public. The chancellor exercised this jurisdiction in his own court which was an ecclesiastical court, administered according to the law of the Church, canon law. He had authority to pronounce excommunication and issue mandates to imprison delinquents. This is confirmed by royal letters directed to the sheriff of Cambridge.[7] This jurisdiction went on for many centuries until it fell into disuse in the eighteenth century and was finally abolished in 1856.

Having through the favour of the bishops of Ely established itself as an ecclesiastical corporation, the university eventually secured its independence of the bishop by having recourse to the papacy. In 1318 Pope John XXII had issued at the request of

6. Charter of Edward I, confirming the privileges of the university, 6 February 1292. The illuminated initial letter E shows the king seated and presenting the charter; kneeling before him are two regent masters wearing the cappa clausa *and hood. They have the tonsure of secular clerks and represent the two proctors of the university. Standing behind them are two doctors with their doctor's caps; the one on the left wears the* pallium, *a cape with two slits for the hands, and is probably a Doctor of Canon Law. The one of the right has a* cappa manicata, *a sleeved cape, and is probably a Doctor of Civil Law. (University of Cambridge Archives)*

17

Edward II a letter addressed to 'his beloved sons of the corporation of Masters and scholars of the *studium generale* of Cambridge of the diocese of Ely',[8] confirming all the privileges of the university and recognizing its status as a *studium generale*; this term had a meaning equivalent to our own term, *university,* and the status of *studium generale* carried with it the valued qualification for its masters of the *ius ubique docendi,* the right to teach everywhere.[9] By the fourteenth century it was felt that such a right required the sanction of the universal authority of the popes, even though the origin of the earliest universities had been spontaneous and had not depended on papal authorisation. The characteristics of a university were considered by then to be the presence of students from distant regions and not just from the locality, a plurality of masters, and teaching not only of arts but in one of the higher faculties, theology, law or medicine. Places like Paris, Bologna, Oxford, Padua and Orleans had all blossomed as universities before obtaining papal recognition; so too had Cambridge. There was but one step from obtaining such recognition from the supreme authority in the Church to claiming exemption from any lower authority, especially that of the bishop. This is what Cambridge finally achieved in 1430.

Archbishop Arundel had carried out a visitation of the university in 1401 as part of the official campaign against Lollardy, but in that year Boniface IX dispensed the chancellor-elect from the obligation of obtaining confirmation from the Bishop of Ely because of the labour and expense involved.[10] The bishops did not accept this tamely and so in 1430 Pope Martin V deputed the Prior of Barnwell to judge the university's claim to possess independent ecclesiastical jurisdiction. The university produced spurious bulls attributed to Honorius I and Sergius I, both of them seventh century popes who reigned long before there was a university anywhere in Europe, and the prior gave judgement in its favour, forbidding archbishops and bishops from interfering in its affairs or examining its members. The decision was confirmed by Eugenius IV in 1433.[11] By the fifteenth century it was clear that universities were too big and too important nationally and even internationally to be considered as an adjunct of a diocese. Seen from this point of view, the papal decisions make sense as they show a regard for the universal good of Christendom which the universities themselves unfortunately did not have the strength or the courage to maintain; in another hundred years they had fallen under an authority far more demanding than that of the local bishop, the authority of the crown as representing the nation state.

The Studies in Medieval Cambridge

One feature of Cambridge scholastic usage which sometimes puzzles outsiders is that whether a student studies an arts or a science subject for his first degree he obtains a B.A. at the end of the course. There is no B.Sc. at Cambridge; so a Cambridge engineer, for instance, is a B.A., a Bachelor of Arts. The origin of this terminology goes back to the Middle Ages when the basic course of study in all universities was called the course in arts because of the early medieval scheme of the seven arts into which all non-sacred knowledge was divided, i.e. grammar, rhetoric, logic, arithmetic, music, geometry, astronomy.

Medieval arts students started their university courses early, at fourteen or fifteen, and were expected to arrive with a good knowledge of Latin. They began with grammar, using the works of Priscian (sixth century A.D.), but this was philosophical grammar, concerned with questions such as the function of parts of speech, the modes of signification and the parallel between the modes of reality and the modes of thought. After that, the basic author was Aristotle, in so far as his works were known in the Middle Ages, the *Physica, De Anima, De generatione et corruptione animalium, De coelo et mundo,* the *Metaphysica* and the *Ethica,* of which only the first three books were known in the West until 1240. Later the *Politics* were added, and by the fifteenth century considerably more mathematics was studied in Cambridge.

The arts course was spread over seven years and the students had to study the books with the help of lectures given by the Masters or Bachelors, who went through the text sentence by sentence, explaining the meaning of the words and expounding the argument of the author. The books were literally read to the students by the teacher since few students were able to afford the textbooks.

Once a good grounding had been given, the student had to acquire the art of rational argument. The disputation was the characteristic exercise of the medieval university; one student, the proponent, argued in favour of a proposition and another, the respondent, argued against it. The debate was presided over by a Bachelor or Master who would in due course *determine* the question, i.e. give his own solution to it. No one could determine until he had been a student for four years and had been accepted by a Master as a Bachelor; such an acceptance, which made a student in effect an associate teacher, allowed him to go on with his own studies for another three years while at the same time teaching the basics to other students and acquiring experience in disputations. Once the three years after *determination* were complete the Bachelor could *incept*, i.e. begin his career as a Master of Arts. In the Middle Ages, to become an accredited university teacher was called to assume the rule, *regimen*, of scholars; the teaching Masters were therefore called *regent* Masters which explains the title *Regent House*, still used in Cambridge for the assembly of teaching members of the university.

After the course in arts, in the medieval sense, a student at Cambridge had the choice of further study in four higher faculties, theology, canon law, civil law and medicine. The faculty of civil law was founded probably about 1240, the faculty of medicine by the end of the century; the origins of the faculty of canon law go back to about 1230 though this date is less sure, and the faculty of theology was also probably in existence by 1230. It seems that most of the masters and scholars who had migrated to Cambridge in 1209 had been 'artists' and the largest faculty at Cambridge, as at Oxford and Paris, during the Middle Ages was that of arts, but the fame of the university depended on the two ecclesiastical faculties, theology and canon law; very few universities in Europe offered both these specialities.

If someone today were asked what he imagined theology teaching to have been like in the Middle Ages, perhaps he might say two things, that it was narrowly authoritarian and that it disregarded the Bible. In fact, the exact opposite is the case in both respects.

The theology course was taught by Bachelors and Masters in theology; the *Sentences* of Peter Lombard (c.1095–1160) was the standard text and the Bachelors *read* it with the students, building a course round it and using it as a framework but not necessarily following Lombard's opinions. The thirteenth century in fact saw the birth of systematic theology, an attempt to study theology scientifically, using the light of reason guided by faith to try to understand as far as possible the truths revealed to man by God, and, in the process, trying to evaluate as sources of information the texts of Scripture, the writings of the Fathers and ecclesiastical tradition. It was a Master's privilege and duty to read, analyse and comment on the Bible in depth. Bachelors also had to read the text *cursorily* as an apprenticeship.

The standard form of teaching, once the *Sentences* had been read, was the disputation. This was a debate, in which Bachelors were the respondents and at which a Master presided. An opinion was enunciated; objections to it were brought forward one by one and answered systematically. Far from being authoritarian, the method was dialectic in the extreme. To read an article of the *Summa Theologica* of St Thomas Aquinas, with its array of objections, its counter arguments and its reasoned conclusion, is to catch the atmosphere of the medieval theological method. After the disputation between the Bachelors, the Master would *determine* the question by giving his solution, either immediately or on the next lecture day. Many of these *determinations* were published under the title of *Questiones disputatae* and they form some of the most novel and interesting theological texts of the Middle Ages. Another form of disputation was the *quodlibet,* a free-for-all (which is more or less what the name means) held in advent and lent at which the Master of Theology himself would be the respondent and take on all comers in argument.

The course in theology was a long one; if the theological student had been a regent Master of Arts, he could begin to oppose in a disputation in his fifth year, but if not, he had to wait until his seventh year. In the seventh year from his regency in arts, he was allowed to *read* the *Book of Sentences* with students and become

21

a Bachelor of Theology. The highest distinction in the academic world then was the degree of Master of Theology. It was obtainable only at Paris, Oxford and Cambridge in the thirteenth century and during the greater part of the fourteenth century. This degree, which was later called the Doctorate in Divinity, was conferred on those who had been regent Master in Arts, who had attended lectures in theology for ten years including two years of lectures on the Bible, who had *read* for students all the books of the *Sentences* and some book of the Bible, who had been opponent and respondent in the theology faculty after reading the *Sentences* and who had preached publicly to the clergy. So it took eighteen years for an M.A. to become Master of Theology; for a friar it was twenty years. But the time could be, and was generally, shortened by one's supplicating for a grace, for which a fee had to be paid. Another title for the Master of Theology was *magister in sacra pagina*, Master of the sacred page, so that the ability to expound the Scriptures was considered as the highest achievement of the theologian. It is important to note that this was the case in the new universities of the thirteenth century because, before they came into being, the study of Scripture had often been considered as the *only* proper study of the theologian; in fact the pre-eminence of Scripture had sometimes been expressed by the apparently related, but really quite different, idea that somehow all human knowledge was present in Scripture. The coming of scholastic theology made it impossible to hold such a view because it had to cope with Aristotle and with metaphysical questions derived from man's understanding of the world and not from the study of Scripture. It might have been expected that, in consequence, Scripture would have been ousted from its central place in Christian theology. This was not the case in the Middle Ages. Giving to human reason its place in religious speculation did not mean denying the importance of God's revelation to man; the supreme achievement of the medieval theologian was considered to be his ability to use all the subtleties of his intelligence, trained by the tradition of the Church, in commenting on the word of God as contained in the Bible. This view of Scripture is expressed in one of the most impressive works of art to have survived from the ages of faith, the windows of King's College Chapel (see below pp. 60–4).

The Friars in Cambridge

The friars brought to the Church in the early thirteenth century a new ideal of religious life. They wanted to give up everything and follow Christ but, unlike the monks, they aspired to do this not in seclusion from the world but in the midst of it. The other great difference between them and the older orders was that they tried to support themselves without having recourse to the feudal system of endowments in lands or rents. They appealed directly to the charity of the faithful; they were *mendicants* as opposed to the *possessionate* orders.

Within this general similarity, there were differences in emphasis. St Francis made poverty and humility in imitation of Christ absolutes for his followers. For Dominic, poverty was a means to an end which was the preaching of the Catholic faith in all its purity. The Carmelites and Austin friars had their origins in groups of hermits which were later assimilated to the mendicant model. Great demands were soon made on all the friars to provide preachers and confessors and so they felt the need to train some of their members in theology. This and the desire to make recruits among students explains their early presence in a university town like Cambridge.

The Franciscans or Greyfriars

The first to come were the Franciscans; the date usually given for their arrival is 1225, during the lifetime of St Francis and a year after their arrival in England. We have a record of their coming in the Chronicle of Brother Thomas, usually called Thomas of Eccleston, which dates from about 1258–9. This is what he says about the first friars in Cambridge:

> At Cambridge the burgesses of the town first received the friars, setting aside for their use the old synagogue which was next to the gaol. However the proximity of the gaol became intolerable for the brothers because the same entrance served for both them and the gaolers; so the Lord King gave twenty marks to buy the rent and thus compensate his Exchequer for the rent of the area. And so the brothers built a chapel so very poor that it took the carpenter one day to make and put

up the fifteen pairs of beams. On the feast of Saint Laurence they sang the Office solemnly in plainchant and there were only three brothers who were clerics, that is Brother W. de Esseby and Brother Hugh de Bugeton and a novice called Brother Elias who was so lame that he had to be carried into the oratory, and as he sang he wept so much that the tears could be seen running down his face. And when he died a most holy death at York, he appeared to Brother W. de Esseby at Northampton and on his asking how he was he replied: 'It goes well with me; pray for me.'[12]

It is to be noted that the friars asked the townsfolk to provide their accommodation; as a result they were settled in the centre of the town, since the house of Benjamin the Jew which was granted to them was probably on the site of the present Guildhall. However the king was also generous to the friars. There are several references to royal alms given for their food and in 1238 Henry III wrote to the burgesses at Cambridge to inform them that he had granted to the friars for the extension of their quarters the whole of the house which had formerly belonged to Benjamin the Jew and had been used as a gaol.

The atmosphere surrounding the first Franciscans was one of great poverty and spiritual fervour. Today it would be called *charismatic* and the tears which ran down Brother Elias's face when they first sang the office at Cambridge are characteristic of those early days. So is the sense of the nearness of the supernatural, conveyed by the story of Brother Elias's appearance in a dream. As for their poverty, it is recorded that the friars of the Cambridge custody (i.e. East Anglia) had no cloaks although they lived in one of the coldest parts of England. The Chronicle also records that when these Franciscan pioneers were really cold they used to huddle together to keep warm *sicut porcis mos est*, 'in the way that pigs do'.[13] With habits such as these, no wonder that the early friars endeared themselves to their contemporaries. Alas, such fervour did not last; and one of the manuscripts of the Chronicle has in the margin a note written in a fifteenth century hand, commenting acidly on what Thomas of Eccleston says about the very poor little chapel at Cambridge: *Nota quod sic non aedificant hodie,* 'N.B. they do not build like that today.'[14]

24

The Cambridge house of the Franciscans soon became a house of studies though it had not started as such. Vincent de Coventry was the first Franciscan to teach theology at Cambridge, probably about 1240. The Chronicle carefully lists the succession of theology lecturers at Cambridge and notes those who had incepted at Paris or Oxford. The others must have taken their theology degree at Cambridge since at that period there was nowhere else where they could have done so. The theology faculty was in existence before the arrival of the friars and was in origin a faculty of secular theologians. The friars, however, soon outnumbered the seculars and during their quarrel with the university in the early fourteenth century they actually claimed that they had founded the theology faculty at Cambridge.[15]

The increase of numbers as the Franciscan house in Cambridge developed as a house of studies must have been one of the factors which determined a move to another site. There were apparently fifty-eight Franciscans in 1277 and in 1289 there were seventy-five, their highest total ever at Cambridge. By 1274 the Franciscans were established in spacious new buildings on the east side of the town on a site provided for them by the townsfolk and occupied today by Sidney Sussex College. The church was a large one, frequently used by the university in later centuries for its assemblies, and there was also a cloister, a refectory and a school house of two storeys. The site covered over three acres and went as far as the King's Ditch, the defence of the town on the southern and eastern sides. On the further side of the Ditch, the friars also had land and an orchard.

The Franciscans in Cambridge were concerned to have a good supply of water; in 1325 they built a conduit from a spring about a mile to the west of Cambridge and brought the water in lead pipes, under the Cam and the old town, to their friary on the east side of Cambridge. A large community obviously needed a plentiful supply of clean water, and in 1350 we find the Carmelites at Cambridge making a similar conduit for their house in Milne Street. After the Reformation the Franciscans' property passed into the hands of Trinity College, and the water which splashes in the splendid Jacobean fountain in Great Court today still flows along the conduit built by them.

The Dominicans or Blackfriars

The Dominicans have left no personal record of their coming to Cambridge which can compare with the Chronicle of the early Friars Minor. All that we have is a series of references in official records; in 1238 Henry III gave four oaks for the building of the Friars Preachers in Cambridge and such gifts follow until 1248, indicating that the priory was being built at that time. In 1240 the Dominicans were allowed to enclose a lane on the south side of their church, and this points to the same conclusion. The origins of the priory are unknown. Alice, widow of Robert de Vere, fifth Earl of Oxford, was a generous benefactress when the buildings were enlarged shortly after 1280. Like the Franciscans, the Dominicans were obviously expanding at Cambridge; royal grants of rations suggest seventy-five Dominicans in 1289 and fifty-five in 1326. The site was large, ten acres outside the medieval town by the Barnwell Gate. It is difficult to say anything about the buildings since these have been almost completely obliterated by Emmanuel College, which now occupies the site; the present hall and combination room were probably contrived within the nave of the friars' church.[16]

The fish pond of the Dominicans still exists in the splendid gardens of the college; another feature, which has disappeared but of which we know from the sources, was the preaching cross or outdoor pulpit at which the friars carried out the main calling of the order; it is probably because of it that the present St Andrew's Street was formerly called Preachers Street.

In the middle of the thirteenth century the Master General of the Dominicans wrote round to all the priors of the order asking them to send in any stories of miracles or edifying happenings which had occurred to the brethren so that the memory might be preserved; from these were compiled the *Vitae Fratrum* which was complete about 1260. There are two edifying tales from Cambridge; one is about Brother William, a lector at the university who appeared after his death to Brother Benet, the sub-prior of Cambridge, wearing a golden crown and accompanied by a man of majestic appearance. Brother Benet questioned him about his state and the companion replied, 'He has already been crowned with one halo and is certain of receiving the rest.' The other story was contributed by Brother Seyer, also teaching at Cambridge; he reported how a certain holy man used often to see a globe of light come down and rest upon the heads of the brethren when they were singing the anthem of Our Lady after compline.[17]

Although these two stories do not contribute the sort of information that we would like to have about the first Dominicans at Cambridge they do give us an insight into their mentality, with its overriding respect for holiness and its sense of the nearness of the supernatural world. There is also the concern to sanction devotion to Mary, since the Dominicans were the foremost at this period in popularising the solemn singing of the *Salve Regina* after compline.[18]

It should not, however, be thought that the early masters in theology at Cambridge were all piety and no learning. We have evidence from the end of the thirteenth century showing that the friars were taking their full part with the secular theologians in the disputations of the faculty. There is a unique manuscript, now at Assisi, which contains an account of Cambridge and Oxford disputations between the years 1282 and 1290.[19] At Cambridge the Dominican, John Trussebut, debates with the Franciscan, John de Letheringset, the question: 'It is asked whether the intellect of man in this life can be so elevated as to see the divine essence, notwithstanding that it is united to physical powers.' Another disputation between Trussebut and a Dominican called Brother Simon is entitled: 'The question is about the Trinity, whether the simplicity of God is compatible with a trinity of persons.' Yet another is: 'It is asked concerning the eminence of knowledge of the soul of Christ whether he knows all things with the simplicity of the Word itself.' The proponent of that question was Ralph Walpole, Archdeacon of Ely; the opponent was William de Erpingham, otherwise unknown but probably a secular clerk. Other topics, concerning the physics of the risen body or the modes of angelic knowledge, would have less appeal today, but the general impression given is that of discussion concerning questions central to the Christian faith and which have not ceased to be debated in the intervening centuries. It is clear that seculars and religious contributed equally to the intellectual life of the faculty of theology at Cambridge during this period. The notes which we have in this manuscript were probably taken by a secular master during his years of training which seem to have begun in Cambridge and continued at Oxford. How the manuscript reached Italy is not known but it is mentioned in a catalogue of books in the Franciscan friary at Assisi in 1381.

The Carmelites or Whitefriars

The Carmelites are an order of friars which derives from groups of hermits living in Mount Carmel in Palestine. Members of this group were introduced to Western Europe by returning Crusaders; their first arrival in England dates from 1242 and in 1249 they are recorded as being at Chesterton, where they still lived as hermits, each with his own cell. In 1256 land was given to them in Newnham, three acres of what was then an island in the fen, surrounded by osier beds and small streams. Here the Carmelites had fishing rights. The isolation of this settlement in the middle of river and marshland would have been ideal for those who wanted to live a contemplative life and yet be close to Cambridge, but the Carmelites adopted a style of life like that of the other friars. In 1267 they were building a church and Henry III gave twelve pairs of rafters for the fabric; we also hear of a cloister and refectory. By 1290 scholars in Cambridge were complaining that they found it difficult because of the floods to go and hear their theology lectures at Newnham, so that by then the house of solitaries had become a house of studies. At about the same period Humphrey de Nekton is recorded as the first member of the order to have taken his degree of Master at Cambridge.

About 1292 the Carmelites moved into the town of Cambridge to a site on Milne Street, a street which ran close to and parallel to the river in the Middle Ages and of which truncated sections survive in Queens' Lane and Trinity Lane. The site is now occupied partly by Queens' College and extended as far as King's College Chapel on the north. Here the friars built a church and conventual buildings of which nothing survives today. They were allowed to enclose their property with two long walls running down to the water's edge, on condition that they made a gate in each wall so that the men of the town could have access to the bank of the river when this was needed for the defence of the town.

There are few details about the life of the Carmelites in Cambridge during the Middle Ages; their numbers have been estimated from the amount of royal alms allocated to the house at an average of thirty-five at the end of the thirteenth century and fifty in the first quarter of the fourteenth century.[20] Important visitors are recorded as staying with them when Parliament met in Cambridge in 1388 and one of the university chests was in their keeping. They were directly involved in one academic row of major proportions in the fourteenth century. John Stokes, a Cambridge Dominican, with a historical sense rare for the period, attacked the claim of the Carmelites to have unbroken continuity as an order going back to the prophet Elijah. He was answered by John de Hornby, a Cambridge Carmelite. In 1374 the Chancellor of the University, John Dunwich, set up a court of regent and non-regent Masters at the request of Hornby to decide whether the Whitefriars could rightly be called *Friars of the Blessed Mary of Mount Carmel*. The Carmelites produced their rule and various papal documents and the court ruled that they could justify their title and could be considered, as it cautiously phrased it, 'imitators and successors of Elijah and Elisha'.[21]

We possess the text of a series of lectures given at Cambridge by one of the Carmelite friars at this period; Thomas Maldon was regent Master round about 1375, after having been the prior of the house. He lectured on the text of Psalm 118 and one of his comments may reflect the controversy on Carmelite origins in its firm allusion to 'Elijah the prophet, father and founder of our order'.[22] His treatment of the text of Scripture shows one of the attractive aspects of the scholastic method in allowing spirituality to flow directly from theology. When discussing original sin, he affirms that Mary was preserved from it by grace; in this he takes his stand with Duns Scotus against St Thomas Aquinas, although in other questions he is frequently influenced by Aquinas.[23]

Another theologian who defended the Immaculate Conception was the Dominican Thomas Hopeman, who was probably lecturing in Cambridge in 1345. He tells the story of an Oxford lecturer who refused to consider 8 December, the feast of Our Lady's Conception, as a holiday and who wanted to lecture then as usual; every year however he was struck down by illness on 8 December until he eventually took the point and rallied to the opinion that Mary was immaculately conceived.[24] In the mid-thirteenth century the friars in Cambridge must have been an intellectually and spiritually attractive group for we have records of other members of the university joining them, such as William de Walcote who resigned his fellowship at King's Hall in 1352 to become a Franciscan.[25]

The Austin Friars

The Austin friars were the last of the friars to come to Cambridge. They too took their origin from a group of hermits, but in central Italy this time, and they were united to form an order under the impulse of the papacy. Their full name is *Order of the Hermits of Saint Augustine* and the year 1256 is usually taken as marking their emergence as an order of friars. The first mention of their house in Cambridge occurs in 1289 in the Roll of Alms of Edward I; Sir Geoffrey Picheford, Constable of Windsor Castle, is referred to as making a property over to them in 1290 and he is considered as the founder of the house; two years later the friars were authorised to enclose their property by two walls running down the King's Ditch where it formed the southern defences of the town (along the line of today's Pembroke Street and Downing Street) on the same conditions as mentioned above in the case of the Carmelites. Other donations of land and houses followed from Cambridge citizens and the Austin friars' property eventually consisted of the whole of the land now covered by the old Cavendish Laboratory and by that complex of laboratories and teaching buildings called the New Museums' Site. The buildings have completely disappeared although one range survived until the eighteenth century (see plate 7).

The house flourished if the calculation of its numbers based on distribution of rations from the king is correct; these indicate that there were approximately twenty friars in 1289 and thirty-six in 1297.[26] Their buildings were used by the university for many of its functions. In fact, the Cambridge house was, with Paris and Oxford, the main *studium generale* of the order. In the middle of the fourteenth century Thomas of Strassburg, prior general of the Austin friars, visited the order in England and it is probable

The Refectory of St Augustins Monastery Cambridge
1780.

7. *Austin Friars. An eighteenth century water colour showing a part of the medieval house of the Augustinian friars, as seen from a window in Corpus Christi College, looking eastwards. The water colour is probably by Michael Tyson, Fellow of Corpus Christi 1767–1780. The building is described as the refectory but is more likely to have been the infirmary or guesthall of the friary. After the Dissolution it was used as a printing house and then became part of the Botanic Garden in the seventeen-nineties before being pulled down.* (University Library: Views X, 2, 70)

that he devised regulations for the house of studies at Cambridge and Oxford as he had done for Paris. His rules for the Paris house still exist;[27] they establish a marked distinction between the academics and the other members of the community in matters of food, observance and timetable.

If similar dispositions were adopted for Cambridge at this time

31

they would explain the strong reaction of which we have evidence in the life and writings of William Flete.[28] He is best known as the spiritual guide and confidant of St Catherine of Siena but his writings throw a welcome shaft of light on the life of the Austin friars at Cambridge in the mid-fourteenth century. We first hear of Flete in 1352 when he was licensed to hear confessions by the Dominican Bishop of Ely, Thomas de Lisle. He must have been at Cambridge by then and in 1359 he was a Bachelor of Theology. He would normally have gone on to a Mastership but in that year he obtained permission to settle at Lecceto, near Siena, one of the centres of Augustinian spirituality where many of the friars still lived a life of solitude in the ilex woods which gave the place its name. There William too adopted a quasi-eremitical state; this fact is itself a commentary on his attitude to the intellectual life, but in addition William Flete spelled out his views in a letter written in 1380 to the Masters in Theology in England:

> You ought to be of assistance to the priors so that everyone, both those who are engaged in study and those who are not, should obey them humbly. You must instruct the students in such a way that they do not lose the substance for the accidents. As they progress in learning, they should take more account of the order and its observances. They should attend divine office with more devotion, as far as place and time permit, and there should be a corresponding progress in virtue otherwise study will lead to their loss. Those who give up the observance of the order for the sake of study lose both their time and their study and will find at the end that they have been deluded and deceived. They should study primarily because of the obedience that has been laid upon them and not because of the degree they are to obtain. To do it all for the sake of the degree is to have an intention which is corrupt.[29]

This is a clear expression of the tension felt between the original ideals of the order and the demands of a house of studies. Since the number of friars who were admitted to theology degrees in any one year was limited by the faculty to one only and since the degree gave rise to many privileges within the house and order, it is obvious that there was a scramble for degrees among the

Austins at Cambridge which severely impaired the religious dedication of the friars.

Almost one hundred years later a set of regulations for the Cambridge *studium* were recorded in the registers of the prior general. They are obviously supplementary to a complete code but what they say gives us an insight into the daily life of student friars at this time.[30] They were to be regular in attending lectures at the university and not to wander about in the town but to go home immediately after lectures unless they had a permission from the prior. The moderator of the *studium* was to arrange three disputations a week within the friary unless there was a disputation at the university. There had obviously been irregularities about access to the library because it is enacted that no one is to have a key to the library without the knowledge of the librarian. Keys must not be loaned or sold to seculars; no one may be admitted to the library to read or write there unless an Augustinian stays with him. The existence of a good library was of immense importance in the Middle Ages, when books were rare and extremely expensive. We have little direct information about the libraries of the friars at Cambridge but there exists a medieval catalogue of the library of the Austin friars at York which lists 646 volumes; it is incidentally a measure of the enormous destruction wrought at the Reformation that only seven of these are known to exist today. York was not a *studium generale* and so we may surmise that the library at Cambridge was considerably larger. Some thirty books from the library have survived and are now in the Vatican Library because someone assembled and packed about two hundred manuscripts from the Cambridge friaries at the time of the Dissolution and shipped them off to Rome, in what condition we do not know.[31] Apart from these, the destruction has been almost complete.[32]

Unfortunately the good relations between the university and the friars were troubled by conflict in the fourteenth century. Similar troubles occurred at Paris and Oxford; obviously the presence of theological schools which claimed the privileges of the university without accepting the authority of the secular regent masters was bound to cause difficulty. It has been estimated that there was something like two hundred friars at Cambridge by 1300; although we have no means of calculating the probable number of secular clergy in the theology schools, it is quite possible that the seculars felt threatened by the numbers of friars. They could also have been jealous of the four splendid friaries, with their new churches; they were like a circle of new buildings around the crowded centre of the old town at a time when the university itself possessed hardly any premises of its own.

In 1303 a university statute was passed which made it a condition for the degree of Master of Theology to have preached a sermon in Great St Mary's; a sermon in one of the friars' churches would not do as heretofore. The friars were furious and appealed to Rome, and the university eventually gave way. The Franciscans and Dominicans stood together on this issue and they were much annoyed that the Augustinian, John de Clare, should have sided with the university.

There was more trouble in 1359 when the university passed a statute making it unlawful for two friars from the same order to incept in the same year and ruling that there should never be two Masters or Bachelors in the same friary lecturing at the same time. Another statute forbade the admission of boys under eighteen into any of the orders. Once again there were appeals to Rome; eventually the friars won on the issue of the age of admission but the limitations on their numbers as regards teaching and incepting were maintained.

The First Colleges

So far we have not said anything about the colleges. This may be surprising to those who know the university as it is today. It is impossible for an undergraduate to study at Cambridge without gaining admission to a college, as thousands of applicants every year well know. Cambridge graduates tend to have an allegiance to their college rather than to the university, as the regular reunions of old members and the flow of donations and legacies indicate, and generous founders are still attracted by the college ideal, as is shown by the foundation of a splendid new college called Robinson College in 1977. Indeed, the magnificent buildings of the colleges, their courts, chapels, gateways, halls and gardens, make Cambridge a favourite place for tourists from all over the world.

This however has not always been the case. In the Middle Ages most students were not members of a college. To acquire the status and privilege in law of being a student it was sufficient to find a Master of Arts who would put the name of a newcomer on his *matricula* or list.[33] This is the origin of the requirement of matriculation for entry into the university. As regards lodgings, some students lived in the house of their master, others in lodgings in the houses of Cambridge citizens, others in hostels which were unendowed lodging houses. One of Chaucer's Canterbury Tales, the Reeve's tale, is about Cambridge students in the fourteenth century and describes some of the adventures that they got up to.[34] Other records allow us to glimpse the violence and drunkenness, the licentiousness, the bawdiness and poverty of student life in the Middle Ages. It is against this background that the foundation of the first colleges took place. Their founders saw them as giving to a few students a privileged opportunity for a more disciplined and regular life, with a modicum of food, housing and clothing deriving from a permanent endowment. But in the Middle Ages only few of the total number of scholars could belong to a college, and of these the majority were graduates.

The term *college* means properly a group of people who own property corporately for a common purpose. Today the word is associated with education and is often used as more or less the equivalent of the word *school*. But in earlier times colleges existed for purposes other than education; for instance, colleges of secular priests were founded to carry out the offices for the dead and in 1483 Richard III founded the College of Arms to regulate the use of heraldry in England.

The colleges of Oxford and Cambridge were founded to unite in a common life groups of masters and groups of students. College life brought them together to pray, either in a nearby parish church or in the chapel of the college, and to have their meals together in the college hall which could also be used for lectures and other gatherings. These medieval ways explain certain aspects of Cambridge life which have survived until today. For instance, the presence of a chapel with regular services in the older colleges and the importance of dining together; today students have the choice of cafeteria-type meals and 'formal hall', but the latter has retained its importance and popularity. There are also college feasts, which were originally celebrations of the feasts in the ecclesiastical calendar, and which have become today opportunities for inter-collegiate academic hospitality of a particularly lavish and formal kind.

The early colleges had what appears today to be a monastic atmosphere because their members were all of them men and all celibate. The Fellows were mostly priests and, even when the law of clerical celibacy disappeared in the Church of England after the Reformation, Fellows were not allowed to marry; this aspect of Cambridge life persisted until 1882, so strong were the demands of college life felt to be. Another feature which reflects medieval usage is the grouping of rooms around a staircase with an open doorway at the bottom. There are no corridors so that residents have to cross the open courtyard to get from one part of the college to another.

The first college to be founded at Cambridge was Peterhouse. In 1280 Hugh de Balsham, Bishop of Ely, obtained a licence to place some scholars into the Hospital of St John the Evangelist. This arrangement, not surprisingly, did not work; four years later the scholars moved to a site outside the Trumpington gate of the town where they bought two houses. Gradually they acquired more property and began to put up their own buildings, beginning with a hall in 1290. But the college never had its own chapel during the Middle Ages and worshipped at the nearby church of St Peter which, from the mid-fourteenth century, has been called St Mary the Less or Little St Mary's.

After the founding of Peterhouse there was a lull until the fourteenth century, when a whole group of colleges were founded at Cambridge. Edward II started the fashion with King's Hall which had the unique status of being an extension of the royal household, training young clerks for the king's service. The warden was appointed by the crown and there were thirty-two scholars, i.e. Fellows, supported by the exchequer, and a number of undergraduates, known in Cambridge as *the king's childer*. Edward II gave them in 1337 a site of their own where part of Trinity College now stands; King Edward's tower in Great Court was originally the entrance to King's Hall from the south[35] and has on it the Plantagenet royal arms, some of the finest heraldry in Cambridge. The members of King's Hall used All Saints' in Jewry as their place of worship until a chapel was built for them in the fourteen-sixties.

It may well be the royal example which caused the foundation of a series of new colleges after King's Hall. Michaelhouse owes its origin to Hervey de Stanton, a priest high in the royal administration who was Chancellor of the Exchequer from 1316 to 1326. He bought a house for scholars and the gift of the living of St Michael's church in 1323. Always a small college, it merged with King's Hall in 1546 to form the nucleus of Henry VIII's foundation of Trinity College. It began with a Master, three M.A.s and two Bachelors of Arts as Fellows; all these had to be students in one of the higher faculties. They used St Michael's church for worship and occupied buildings on the south side of the present Great Court of Trinity.

Clare and Pembroke were both founded by aristocratic ladies of great wealth. Elizabeth de Clare, daughter and co-heiress of the sixth Earl of Gloucester, began in 1336 a series of benefactions which transformed a struggling house of studies for theologians and logicians, called University Hall, into Clare Hall, the forerunner of the present day Clare College. In 1359 a new set of statutes for the college provided that, in addition to the graduate members of the foundation, there should be some poor boys, who were to study grammar. The members of Clare Hall worshipped at first in the nearby parish church of St John Zachary, a building which was later pulled down to make room for King's College Chapel, but in 1348 Lady de Clare obtained from the pope a licence to build in her college a chapel, another innovation which later became the norm.[36]

The same elements are found in Pembroke College, founded in 1347 by Marie de Valence, Countess of Pembroke; grammar school boys are to be on the foundation and in 1355 Innocent VI grants to the master and scholars of 'Valense Mary Hall' license to celebrate the divine office in their own chapel;[37] up till then they had used the church of St Botolph.

Gonville Hall and Trinity Hall both owe their origin to clerics. Edmund Gonville, a secular priest and holder of several livings in Norfolk, founded Gonville Hall in 1348; its Fellows were to study civil and canon law, medicine and theology but it only had a small endowment and in the Middle Ages its Fellows numbered fewer than the twenty envisaged in the statutes. William Bateman, Bishop of Norwich, founded Trinity Hall in 1350; the foundation statutes mention twenty Fellows, all of them to study canon law and civil law, but here again that number was never reached during the Middle Ages.

Corpus Christi College, as has been mentioned above (page 8), was founded by two of the guilds of the town of Cambridge. Its first statutes date from 1356. They allow for a Master and two Fellows, but, as gifts came in, more fellowships were added. All its members were to be in priest's orders and it was only after a hundred years of its existence that junior members were admitted to the College. Corpus Christi used the nearby church of St Benet for its worship and was usually referred to as Benet College. In the Middle Ages it was reached by a narrow lane past the tower of St Benet's giving access to a low doorway, in marked contrast to the lofty gates of more prestigious foundations. Behind lay the court which then constituted the whole of the college; it was built in the second half of the fourteenth century and is now the oldest complete medieval court of either university, representing very well the small scale of early collegiate building (see plate 8). Corpus Christi College is still surrounded by narrow lanes and buildings in the centre of the town and this gives a good idea of how cramped the premises of all the colleges were in the Middle Ages. The early buildings of St Catharine's and Peterhouse were hidden from Trumpington Street by houses, and between the Old Schools and Great St Mary's there were crowded houses and streets. Gradually the colleges acquired adjacent tenements and pulled them down to make way for their courts and buildings. In the eighteenth and nineteenth centuries came the taste for the open spaces and lawns which now set off to advantage many of the medieval buildings of Cambridge, but this was a much later

8. Corpus Christi College: Old Court. The north range of the court which was built in the second half of the fourteenth century. Behind it is seen the Saxon tower of St Benet's Church; the members of the college worshipped in this church before they had a chapel of their own and the college is frequently referred to until the eighteenth century as Benet College.

The dormer windows and the chimneys were added c. 1530 within the original roof. As planned, the court comprised six staircases with twenty sets of rooms. The open doorways at the foot of each staircase are characteristic of college life; as there are no corridors, residents have to cross the courtyard to get from one part of the building to the other. (Photograph by Andrew Gough)

39

embellishment. In the Middle Ages King's College Chapel must have towered above the houses of the town in the way that many French cathedrals do today. On the river side there was more room but beyond the hythes lay water meadows and marshland, liable to frequent floods, and it is only relatively recently that the colleges have created along the river the gardens, known collectively as *The Backs,* which are, as a group, unrivalled in England.

The statutes of the early colleges show that these small societies were envisaged by their founders as places where prayer for their deceased benefactors would always continue. So William Bateman at Trinity Hall lays down that members of the college shall pray daily for his father and mother, for himself and for his predecessors as bishops of Norwich. The exact number of prayers was laid down; the *De profundis* with *Kyrie eleison,* one Our Father and one Hail Mary, the collect beginning *Inclina Domine* with the mention of his parents, William and Margery, by name, and the collect *Deus qui inter apostolicos* for the founder after his death.[38] Seen from this point of view, the colleges were like chantries and some took the idea further by endowing fellowships for chantry priests, as Queens' did in the fifteenth century.

Colleges also owned splendid vestments, service books and sacred vessels for use at mass and the divine office. Several inventories of these survive but, alas, all the objects designed for Catholic worship which are described in them were destroyed at the Reformation. A late fourteenth century inventory from Corpus Christi College, for instance, mentions, among other items, the white chasuble embroidered with white silk and with gold dragons and cocks embroidered on it, together with a set for deacon and subdeacon. [39] These are among the vestments which are described as being for use in the church (of St Benet) but belonging to the college and not to the parish; there had obviously been some recrimination in the past, hence the need for precision. Also mentioned are two antiphonals with the plainchant for mass. They were a pair but one was marked .S. (*sinistra*) for use on the left hand side of choir and the other .D. (*dextra*) for use on right hand side. The inventory explains that they were for the three masses with plainchant which the Fellows of the college have to celebrate.[40] The college owned no less than six chalices and a *tabernaculum* (we would say a monstrance) of silvergilt worth twenty pounds, 'in which the body of Christ is wont to be carried on solemn days and especially on the day of Corpus Christi'.[41]

The University in the Late Middle Ages

It must not be thought that only the colleges were expanding and building; towards the end of the fourteenth century the university was for the first time in a position to put up its own premises. Up till then its teaching was done in rented houses, but a series of donations had provided property in that part of the town to the west of Great St Mary's. Here the university began to build what is now called the Old Schools. A print made by Loggan in the late seventeenth century shows its appearance as it had been since the Middle Ages and before a classical front was added by the architect Stephen Wright in 1754. Plate 9 reproduces Loggan's engraving, taken from the east, i.e. from the tower of Great St Mary's. The north range, on the right, is the oldest and was completed in 1400; it housed the theology school on the ground floor and above a noble room, now called the University Combination Room, which was the centre of the late medieval university. It was called the Regent House and university business was conducted in it. With its fine proportions (28 feet wide and over 90 feet long) it was the largest room in Cambridge, apart from churches, and must have made the secular clerks feel that they had caught up at last with the buildings of the friars. At the east end stood an altar, so that the whole room could be used as a chapel. Nearest to the altar were stalls for the regent masters who held their deliberations here; a screen, which must have been like the rood screen of a parish church, separated them from the non-regent masters who met at the western end of the room. The medieval ceiling of this magnificent room is still in position, though it had later plaster-work added to it, and the windows on the south and west are original (see plate 10).

The western range, at the further end of the court, contained the school of canon law below and a library above; it was in existence by 1438. On the left was the southern range with the school of civil law on the ground floor and another library above;

41

it was built between 1458 and 1471. The fourth side of the court, the one nearest to the spectator in Loggan's print, was completed in the last years of the fifteenth century through the benefactions

9. *The Old Schools: Loggan's Engraving. This print, from the engraving by David Loggan 1688, shows the Old Schools as they were from the end of the Middle Ages until the addition of a classical facade by Stephen Wright in 1754. In the north range (right) was the theology school on the ground floor and the Regent House above. Canon law was taught on the ground floor in the west range (furthest from the spectator) and above was the library. The east range (nearest to the spectator) was built by Thomas Rotherham, Chancellor of the University, and later Bishop of Lincoln and Archbishop of York. It has a fine decorated archway; the ground floor housed the university's court room and above was a restricted access library, containing the more precious books. The close-set windows of the facade were designed to give maximum light to this library.*

of Thomas Rotherham, Chancellor of the University, Bishop of Lincoln and subsequently Archbishop of York. The ground floor contained the court room where the chancellor's jurisdiction was exercised and above was another library which housed the more precious books and was of restricted access. Its close-set windows, clearly seen in Loggan's picture, were designed to give the maximum light to readers. Rotherham, who was considered one of the principal benefactors of the university, gave many volumes, a princely gift since all these books were manuscripts and immensely costly. The fine gateway which completed the building was also his gift; it is surmounted with the royal arms and is flanked with four niches which we see in their post-Reformation emptiness but which must have contained statues, perhaps of the four Doctors of the Western Church. The completion of this building marked the apogee of the medieval university and we can regret its disappearance behind Wright's facade, elegant though it is.

In the medieval university, processions were important; they were an expression of the corporate nature of the academic body and of its common faith. Permission had to be obtained if someone wanted to be dispensed from attending. There were three general processions which were penitential, or at least impetratory in character, begging for God's mercy; they were held on the first Friday in advent, the Friday before Passion Sunday and the Friday before the Ascension. Other penitential processions might be enjoined for the safety of the king or of the realm. The order of processions was laid down; first came the parish chaplains in surplices with their crosses. They were the priests who actually did the parish work, since vicars and rectors were absentees who drew the revenues. Then came the four orders of friars in their religious habits and always in this order: the Augustinians, the Carmelites, the Franciscans and the Dominicans. After them came the brothers of the Hospital of St John the Evangelist. Then followed the university in academic dress, the bachelors, the chaplains, the regent masters, the non-regents and finally came the people. It must have been a fine sight and the singing of the litanies would have resounded in the narrow streets with their overhanging upper stories as in a tunnel.

Once a year came a great festive procession for the feast of Corpus Christi. This involved the corporation as well as the university and lighted tapers were carried, accompanying the Master of Corpus Christi College holding the monstrance with the Host. The procession went as far as the Great Bridge (Magdalene Bridge) then returned to the college where a feast was held in the evening. Characteristically, the feast survives until this day although the procession has gone. There were also smaller processions in honour of the Blessed Sacrament organised by a parish,[42] so that life must have been colourful at times.

On 26 May 1449 Master John Carawey, priest, made a will; it gives us an interesting insight into the academic and religious society of his time.[43] Master John was the nephew of another priest, also called John Carawey, who had become a commoner at King's Hall in the early part of the century and who, after becoming an M.A. and a Bachelor of Canon Law, had received the living of St Vigor's Church, Fulbourn.[44] He had left all his books to his nephew. We do not know anything about young John Carawey's career, except that he was one of the four Fellows of 'the Queen's College of St Margaret and St Bernard' when this was founded by Margaret of Anjou in 1448.[45]

The President of the new college was Andrew Doket, whose original foundation of a College of St Bernard in 1446 was taken over and refounded by the queen; when the Lancastrian dynasty fell, he persuaded the new queen, Elizabeth Woodville, to extend her patronage to the college and to add to its endowment, so that it became *Queens' College*. Doket, who was rector of St Botolph's church in Cambridge, was a remarkable man to have provided the driving force for the foundation of a new college; he was not wealthy but he obtained benefactions from rich townsmen and, as we have seen, he was able to interest royalty in his project. His monument is the old court of Queens', finished by about 1454, which is a perfect example of medieval collegiate planning (see plate 12); the buildings are of brick, now mellowed to a lovely colour, and it is right that the keystone of the arch of the gateway in Queens' Lane should be a carved figure of Doket, holding the charter of foundation. In the vault of the gateway are bosses of St Margaret and St Bernard (see plate 13), the patrons of the

10. The Regent House: interior looking east. The Regent House was the room where the business of the medieval university was conducted by the regent and non-regent masters. The room was completed before 1400; the gothic windows at the side and the wooden ceiling are original. Plasterwork was inserted into the medieval ceiling c. 1600 and the classical window at the east end replaces the original traceried window shown in Loggan's print. There was originally an altar at the east end of the room and a screen divided the regent masters' stalls from the non-regents who met at the western end of the room. It is now the University Combination Room. (Photograph by Alan Rooke)

college. Carawey made Doket one of the executors of his will and left him a book of devotions and a breviary; the breviary was to be sold and the money used for prayers for John and his uncle (who had given it to him), presumably by being used for mass offerings.

The other executors were Thomas Carawey, not otherwise

known, and Geoffrey Bisshop, also a Master of Arts. He received an iron stove under the will;[46] in the icy climate of Cambridge that must have been one of the most useful aids to study that one can imagine. The *supervisor* of the will was William Wylflete,[47] M.A. and Master of Clare Hall. He was given a pair of prayer books. At the time he was rector of All Saints', Fulbourn, an appointment in which he was succeeded by Geoffrey Bisshop whose memorial brass is still in Fulbourn today.

John Carawey left twenty shillings to his mother and all the books which had come to him from his uncle to 'the new College of St Bernard'; unfortunately he does not tell us the titles of this collection nor its extent, but he does say that the gift was made so that his soul and the soul of his uncle should be prayed for in perpetuity at the college. Every priest attending his funeral was to receive four pence. The rest of his legacies were all in lots of three shillings and fourpence (a sixth of a pound) to the high altar of St Vigor's, to the fabric of that church where he asked to be buried in the sanctuary; to the high altar of St Botolph's, to the Austin friars, to John Depyng, one of the friars there, and to the Abbess of Denney, the house of Franciscan nuns near Cambridge.

Probate was granted on 5 June 1449 before the Vice-Chancellor of the University, who was the Carmelite, Nicholas de Swaffham,

11 (opposite). The Gateway: Madingley Hall. When the east facade of the Old Schools was re-built in 1754 the gateway was sold by the Vice-Chancellor and bought by Sir John Hynde Cotton, squire of Madingley, for £10.10s.0d. Parts of Rother-ham's gateway can be seen in the gateway to the stable courtyard at Madingley Hall. The ogee arch is of a different profile from that shown in Loggan's print but the royal arms above are clearly recognisable; they are the arms of the Yorkist dynasty with two lions as supporters and the sun's rays surrounding the lion of the crest, indicating that Rotherham's facade was completed before the accession of the Tudors in 1485. The four niches were also part of the Old Schools facade and it is suggested that they originally contained the statues of the four doctors of the Western Church (St Gregory, St Ambrose, St Augustine and St Jerome). (Photograph by Alan Rooke)

Doctor of Theology. His court sat in the house of the Carmelite friars which was next door to 'the new College of St Bernard'.

The picture of late medieval Cambridge afforded by this text is one of a close-knit community involving the Fellows, the parish priests and the friars in constant and apparently friendly relationships. Tensions there must have been, as in any human group, but John Carawey's will, made so shortly before his death, allows us to see this little society *sub specie aeternitatis* and in a fairly amiable light.

12. Queens' College: aerial view. Photograph taken from the south east on 5 September 1975. The old court of Queens' College is in the foreground of the picture; the gatehouse faces on to Queens' Lane (the old Milne Street) in the centre of the eastern range of the court. To the north is the old chapel (now the library) with a large traceried window facing the street. The old library occupies the rest of the north range. The hall is on the west side with an oriel window giving on to the court; the south and east ranges are occupied by sets of rooms. The old court of Queens' College, built between 1448–1454, is a perfect example of medieval collegiate planning. It has become the nucleus of later development. To the west is the Master's Lodge and Cloister Court. Beyond the Cam is Cripps Court, 1971-74. To the north of the old court, on land where the Carmelite friary once stood, is the Victorian chapel designed by Boddley in 1890 and the cubic design of Basil Spence's Friars building.

Notes and References to Chapter 2

1. For the history of the university, apart from the general sources mentioned in the notes to the previous chapter, we have relied on Fr Michael Hackett's *The Original Statutes of Cambridge University* (Cambridge, 1970) which has completely renewed the understanding of the origins of the university. For the friars, we have followed J. R. H. Moorman, *The Grey Friars in Cambridge* (Cambridge, 1952), W. Gumbley, *The Cambridge Dominicans* (Oxford, 1938) and F. Roth, *The English Austin Friars* (New York, i, 1966; ii, 1961); for the history of the colleges, we have used B. Little, *The Colleges of Cambridge* (London, 1973).

2. For instance the Peterborough Chronicle: '*Mccix. Scolares recedunt ab Oxonia*'. *Chronicon Petroburgense* (London, Camden Society 1849), p. 6.

3. '*... recessunt ab Oxonia ad tria millia clericorum, tam magistri quam discipuli, ita quod nec unus ex omni universitate remansit; quorum quidam apud Cantabregge, quidam vero apud Radigum, liberalibus studiis vacantes villam Oxonie vacuam reliquerunt*', Roger de Wendover, *Flores Historiarum*, edited by H. G. Hewlett, (RS, 1887), ii, p. 51.

4. H. Rashdall, *The Universities of Europe in the Middle Ages*, edited by F. M. Powicke and A. B. Emden (Oxford, 1936), iii, p. 34.

5. M. B. Hackett, *Original Statutes*, p. 46.

6. *Ibidem*, pp. 153–7.

7. *Ibidem*, p. 272, n. 3.

8. '*Johannes Episocopus, servus servorum dei, dilectis filiis Universitatis Magistrorum et Scolarium studii generalis Cantebrigie, Eliensis diocesis*', quoted from A. B. Cobban, 'Edward II, Pope John XXII and the University of Cambridge', *Bulletin of the John Rylands Library* 47 (1964), p. 77. The form of the name of the town is to be noted. Cantebrige first appears in documents of the latter part of the twelfth century and is used as well as the older form, Grantebrige (see above p. 3), until about 1400 when the older form disappears; *Cantabrigia* remains the usual Latin form and, as such, it still appears today

13 (opposite). Queens' College: boss of St Bernard. Roof boss in the vault of the gatehouse of the front court of Queens' College, 1448. It shows St Bernard, one of the patrons of the college, in the voluminous white cowl of a Cistercian, holding an abbot's crozier in his right hand and the book of the rule of St Benedict in his left. The colouring is modern, reproducing the scheme of colouring devised by George C. Drinkwater in 1934.

Andrew Doket, rector of St Botolph's, was warden of a hostel of St Bernard which stood next to his church. In 1446 he founded a college for which he kept the dedication and this became 'the Queen's College of St Margaret and St Bernard' when refounded by Queen Margaret of Anjou in 1448. The two patron saints are portrayed in the vault above the old entrance to the college in Queens' Lane. (Photograph by Andrew Gough)

50

in abbreviation after letters indicating a Cambridge degree, e.g. B.A. Cantab., M.A. Cantab. The modern form, Cambridge, does not occur in documents until after 1400. The river was still for a time called the Granta but, by a phenomenon which the historians of words call *back-formation*, it came to be called the Cam; Cam as a river name does not occur until about 1600. See J. Willis Clark and A. Gray, *Old Plans of Cambridge 1574 to 1798,* (Cambridge, 1921), p. xii.

9. M. B. Hackett, *Original Statutes,* pp. 178–9.

10. Bull *Dum attentae* of Boniface IX, 1401; see CPR, v, pp. 370–1 and M. B. Hackett, *Original Statutes,* pp. 107–8.

11. CPR, vii, pp. 484–5.

12. *Fratris Thomae vulgo dicti de Eccleston Tractatus de adventu Fratrum Minorum in Angliam,* edited by A. G. Little (Manchester, 1951), p. 22. Translation ours.

13. *Ibidem,* p.12.

14. *Ibidem,* p. 22.

15. This claim was accepted by A. G. Little, 'The Friars and the Foundation of the Faculty of Theology in the University of Cambridge', *Mélanges Mandonnet* (Paris, 1930), ii. pp. 398–400, but see the argument against in M. B. Hackett, *Original Statutes,* p. 132 and n. 2.

16. F. W. Stubbings, 'The Church of the Cambridge Dominicans', *Proceedings of the Cambridge Antiquarian Society* 62 (1969), pp. 97 and 102, argues that the hall and combination room represent the whole of the church but this would give an overall length of 112 feet which is too small for a community of such a size. The traces of an altar which were observed during the repairs to the combination room in the eighteenth century, if such they were, could have been those of a nave altar.

17. *Lives of the Brethren of the Order of Preachers 1206–1259,* translated by Placid Conway, O. P. (London, 1924), pp. 49 and 257.

18. W. R. Bonniwell, *A History of Dominican Liturgy 1215–1945* (New York, 1945), pp. 148–66.

19. A. G. Little and F. Pelster, *Oxford theology and theologians c.A.D. 1282–1302* (Oxford, 1934), pp. 11–13.

20. Keith J. Egan, 'The Establishment and Early Development of the Carmelite Order in England' (unpublished Ph.D. dissertation, University of Cambridge, 1965), p. 145.

21. Quoted in VCH, ii, p. 284.

22. J. P. H. Clark, 'Thomas Maldon, O. Carm., A Cambridge Theologian of the Fourteenth Century', *Carmelus* 29 (1982), p. 194.

23. *Ibidem,* p. 214 and n. 79.

24. S. L. Forte, 'Thomas Hopeman O. P. (c.1350); An Unknown Biblical Commentator', *Archivum Fratrum Praedicatorum* 25 (1955), p. 341. He tells the story about Alexander Nequam (1157–1217); cf. *BRUO,* pp. 1342–3.

25. See *BRUC,* p. 610. Cf. also A. B. Cobban, *The King's Hall within the University of Cambridge in the Later Middle Ages* (Cambridge, 1969), p. 294.

26. F. Roth, *The English Austin Friars,* ii, pp. 51*, 70*–71*, n. 55.

27. See E. Ypma, 'Le "Mare Magnum"; un code médiéval du couvent augustinien de Paris'. *Augustiniana* 6 (1956), pp. 275–321.

28. For William Flete, see especially M. B. Hackett, 'The Spiritual Life of the English Austin Friars of the Fourteenth Century', in *Sanctus Augustinus: Vitae Spiritualis Magister* 2 (1959), pp. 471–92.

29. *Ibidem,* p. 486. Translation ours.

30. The entry is dated 16 November, 1438; see F. Roth, *The English Austin Friars,* ii, pp. 321*–2*.

31. N. R. Ker, 'Cardinal Cervini's Manuscripts from the Cambridge Friars' in *Xenia Medii Aevi Historiam Illustrantia oblata Thomae Kaeppeli O. P.* (Rome, 1978), pp. 52 and 66–9.

32. N. R. Ker, *Medieval Libraries of Great Britain,* second edition (London 1964), lists fourteen manuscripts from the libraries of the Cambridge friaries known to be in Great Britain today.

33. See M. B. Hackett, *Original Statutes,* pp. 72–4.

34. See J. A. W. Bennett, *Chaucer at Oxford and at Cambridge* (Oxford, 1974).

35. It was moved to its present position when Great Court was created in the early seventeenth century, having stood originally where the sundial now is.

36. CPR, iii, p. 269.

37. CPR, iii, p. 562.

38. *Statutes of Trinity Hall Cambridge,* p. 428.

39. M. R. James, 'The Earliest Inventory of Corpus Christi College', *Proceedings of the Cambridge Antiquarian Society,* n. s. 10 (1912), pp. 109–10.

40. *'pro tribus missis cum nota quas oportet socios collegii dicere'; ibidem,* p. 99.

41. *'in quo solet corpus christi differri in diebus solempnibus et precipue in die corporis christi'; ibidem,* p. 111.

42. See for instance the description of such a procession in Cambridge on 30 June, 1389, in F. Roth, *The English Austin Friars*, ii, pp. 240*–1*.

43. ULC, Archives of Queens' College; QC 30.

44. For the known biographical details of the persons mentioned in connection with John Carawey's will, see BRUC, *sub nomina.*

45. *Calendar of Patent Rolls:* Henry VI, v, 1446–1452 (London, 1909), p. 143. Licence dated 30 March, 1448.

46. *'unum caminum de ferro';* ULC, QC 30, r. 6.

47. That is the form of the name in BRUC. In the will the name is spelled Wulflet and Ulflete.

three:

St John Fisher and the Catholic Reform

The last quarter of the fifteenth century seemed to usher in a golden age for Catholic Cambridge.[1] In material terms, it was in the years between about 1480 and 1520 that both town and university acquired so many of their best and most celebrated buildings. But it was as a centre of learning and piety that Cambridge now enjoyed one of its greatest periods; only now could it be said to have caught up with Oxford in prestige. It was at the heart of the new Christian humanism of the Renaissance and this evolution was accomplished with the enthusiastic support of established authorities, both royal and episcopal. Many buildings and institutions familiar to later centuries now appeared in a relatively short space of time. After the foundation of King's in 1446 and Queens' in 1448, there was a lull in the creation of new colleges until St Catharine's was founded by a Provost of King's in 1473. About the year 1478 work began on the complete rebuilding of the university church of Great St Mary's and this created the fabric that is so celebrated a part of later Cambridge. It was completed in 1519 apart from the tower, which was not

14. The statue of St John Fisher on the Divinity Faculty, St John Street, designed by Basil Champney, and opened in 1879. One of eight statues put into the niches of the facade between 1890–8. They represent Fisher, Erasmus, Cranmer, Matthew Parker, John Lightfoot, Benjamin Whichcote, Bishop Pearson and J. B. Lightfoot. The statue shows Fisher the Don, in a furred gown; another nineteenth-century statue, showing Fisher the Bishop, is on p. 119. (Photograph by Andrew Gough).

55

finished until 1608. Another long drawn out piece of work was the construction of a magnificent new gatehouse for King's Hall, between about 1490 and 1535; this survives as the great gate of Trinity College with later additions like the statues of Henry VIII and James I.

It has been justly said that in these years central Cambridge must have resembled nothing so much as a builder's yard, but there was little new about that. There had been great periods of building and founding colleges before—between 1320 and 1352, or between 1428 and 1450. New trends, however, characterise this period as one of Catholic reform. It was not a revolutionary movement, since it was led by bishops and members of the court, but it was radical. For instance, it was prepared to accept that many religious houses fell far short of their original aims. Reformers of undoubted Catholic orthodoxy were sometimes sufficiently pessimistic to denounce all English monks and friars as wordly, excepting only the Franciscan Observants, the Carthusians and the Bridgettines. The reformers were also prepared to dissolve religious houses that no longer served any purpose and to divert their endowment to worthier uses. This was the background to the establishment of Jesus College, founded by Bishop John Alcock of Ely after he had dissolved the nunnery of St Radegund

15 (opposite). Great Saint Mary's from Market Street. The Church of St Mary next to the market has always been at the centre of the life of the university and of the town at Cambridge. In the early years of the university, before it had premises of its own, convocation met in this church, disputations were held in it and degrees conferred there; the university's muniments were kept in the tower and the ringing of the church bells for divine office was used to regulate the times for lectures. This view shows the church as seen from the busy street leading to the market and gives an idea of the crowded medieval town, although the buildings seen in the present-day Market Street are from a later period.

The nave of the church was rebuilt at the beginning of the sixteenth century; the close set clerestory windows are typical of East Anglian Perpendicular churches. The upper storey of the tower was not completed until 1608. (Photograph by Alan Rooke)

which by then comprised only two nuns, one of whom led a scandalous life. Shortly afterwards the Hospital of St John the Evangelist was suppressed to permit the establishment of St John's College.

Nothing could be further from the truth than to imagine that the religious establishment in early Tudor England was complacent or obscurantist. A characteristic figure of Cambridge at this period was William Melton, who obtained his M.A. in 1480 and a Doctorate of Theology in 1496, the year after becoming Master of Michaelhouse. In 1496 he became Chancellor of the diocese of York, where he preached a sermon to those who were candidates for holy orders which was printed by Wynkyn de Worde about 1510. It is highly critical of the ignorance of the clergy; a priest's office was one of the highest dignity and responsibility, he said, yet it had been degraded by boorish and stupid clerics who wasted their time in hunting, drinking and immorality. No Lutheran reformer could have written a more thorough-going denunciation and yet Melton was working for reform within the structure of the Church and his diocesan office gave him the power to take practical measures for improving the education of the clergy.

Melton was especially important because his pupils at Michaelhouse included John Fisher (1469–1535) who became a Fellow in 1491, was a Proctor of the University in 1494–1495 and who succeeded Melton as Master in 1497; with Alcock he helped to raise the money for rebuilding Great St Mary's and it was in this capacity that he made the acquaintance in 1495 of Lady Margaret Beaufort, the mother of King Henry VII. In 1501 Fisher took his D.D. and became the Chaplain of Lady Margaret; in 1502 he was the first of the Lady Margaret Readers of Divinity in Cambridge. Other offices followed, Chancellor of the University in 1504, Bishop of Rochester in the same year and, from 1505 to 1508, President of Queens'. Under Henry VII there were the closest possible links between the court, the reforming clergy and scholars; the early career of John Fisher exemplified this.

The Catholic reformers, anxious for the improvement of the education of the clergy, were able to put into practice a part of their programme in the form of two model colleges where the New Learning could be a part of the curriculum; Christ's was established in 1505 with St John's following in 1511, two years after the death of Lady Margaret but very much in accordance with her intentions and supervised by her steward, Hugh Ashton, Bachelor of Canon Law of Cambridge. Both were on the sites of dissolved foundations, the College of God's House, which had moved from Milne Steet, and the Hospital of St John respectively. As a memorial of this great age of renewed scholarship we have four of the finest buildings in Cambridge—the splendid gatehouses of Trinity, Jesus, Christ's and St John's, all built between 1490 and 1530. It was to a Cambridge almost recognisable in its modern form that King Henry VII travelled in 1506 with Lady Margaret and members of the court. The party was escorted into Cambridge by the civic and county dignitaries and welcomed both by the monks and friars and by the members of the university. Fisher made a speech of welcome at Preachers Street near Christ's and the next day he celebrated mass in King's before the party moved on to Walsingham. Clearly there was no conflict between the new humanism and the old Catholicism as far as Fisher was concerned.

The coming of the new skills and studies was illustrated by the sojourn of Erasmus at Cambridge between 1511 and 1514. He already had friends from the university, men like Richard Foxe, William Blount (Lord Mountjoy) and Thomas Ruthall, Keeper of the Privy Seal (1516), later Bishop of Durham (1509–1523) and Chancellor of the University in 1503–4. Once again we get a picture of a cultured and forward-looking circle among influential men in Church and State. Erasmus came to England at the invitation of Thomas More but he soon moved from London to Cambridge where he stayed at Queens' College, where Fisher had been President since 1505, although he no longer resided in Cambridge since becoming Bishop of Rochester in 1504. Erasmus lectured in Greek and Divinity, just possibly as Lady Margaret Professor, and his chief efforts at this time were directed towards the preparation of his Greek New Testament and of Jerome. He also translated into Latin Greek works, both classical and patristic; and he prepared schoolbooks for the teaching of Latin and Greek. It is appropriate that soon after his departure the university established a Greek lectureship; it was no doubt because of the university's acceptance of his methods that in 1516 Erasmus could describe it as *flourishing,* a word he used sparingly. Asham would soon write of the zeal with which Greek was being studied in Cambridge.

It should be remembered that this enthusiasm for the New Learning took place in the framework of a deeply orthodox community. Perhaps the greatest work of art in Cambridge is to be found in King's College Chapel, where the windows perfectly express this combination—the Renaissance allied to the Catholic faith. King's chapel exhibits an impressive unity of conception; the plan is extremely simple, a vast rectangle with twelve windows on the north and south sides filling all the space between the arches which support the vault. With the east window, there are twenty-five windows devoted to a single theme, since the west window has nineteenth century glass. The theme is the salvation wrought by the life, death and resurrection of Christ, prepared by God's choice of Mary to be the mother of the Redeemer, and working itself out in the life of the Church as shown by the preaching of the apostles, the Assumption of Mary and her Coronation as Queen of Heaven. New Testament scenes are associated in the side windows with scenes from the Old Testament; for instance in the third window from the west on the north side, the Annunciation is below the temptation of Eve; the birth of Christ is below the appearance of God in the burning bush, the bush which burns without being consumed being the symbol of Mary who becomes a mother without ceasing to be a virgin. In the central light of each window there are angels, prophets and

16 (opposite). Signature of St John Fisher on the Statutes of St John's College. The second statutes of the college date from 1530. After the last paragraph of the statutes, written in a fine italic hand, comes the confirmation by John Fisher in the name of the executors of Lady Margaret Beaufort whose legacy made possible the foundation of the College in 1511. This confirmation is written by Master John Bere, notary public, whose mark is drawn in the right margin. It begins In *dei nomine Amen. Nos Joannes permissione divina Roffensis* epus: *'In the name of God, Amen. We John, by divine permission, Bishop of Rochester.' At the foot of the page is St John Fisher's signature:* Jo [annes] Roffensis. (St John's College Archives)

46

...bunt stipendia que socijs conferenda sunt. hec omnia fiant priusq̃ ex numero scholasticorum quisq̃ imminuatur. q̃ si modis istis et hijs subtractionibus collegium ad pristinum statum reduci queat bene fuerit. sin minus tunc iocalia venundentur et ornamenta quibus facilius carere possunt. postea discipulorum numerus qui pro fundatrice sunt instituti quantum ad collegij statum et diuturandum existetur. ampliatior fiat et sane potius ex numero discipulorum qui pro funda-trice instituti sunt imminuendum censeo q̃ ex alijs qui per peculiares fundatores sunt ordinati non solum ob periculum imminebit ex indebtis et oblitacionibus quibus collegium peculiari-bus fundatoribus astringitur. verumenam q̃ ob fauorem quem erga fundatricem idem affecti fuerant liberatius tam liberalem collegio fecerint donationem. postremo si nec istis modis reparari damnum valeat ex aliquot collegij socijs pro fundatrice institutis. id fieri permitti-mus donec ad vberiorem statum vel benignissimi dei vel piorum hominum opitulationibus collegium restitui possit. quo facto volumus vt vnumquodq̃ subtractorum ordine suo per ma-gistri industriam reponi curetur.

In dei nomine Amen. Nos Joannes permissione divina Roffensis & proui nus executorum Illustrissime vnquam domine Margarete Richemondie, Derbieq̃ Comitis nore et autoritate relevorum exea-torum eiusdem principis pariter et iura legee et statuta in hunc libellum redacta ob ampliandum optimi maximi dei cultum, atq̃ sacrarum lit-terarum ac doctrinarum omnium incrementum insistenta pro veritate indubitatib collegij sancti Joannis Euangeliste in Cantabrigia statu-imus habeievolumus et decernimus quibus magistrum et scolac omnes tam socios q̃ discipulos non solum eos qui iam sunt verum etiam ceteros omnes quoique in posterum futuri sunt obnoxios esse atq̃ inuiolabiliter obedire debere per hoc present scriptum declaramus Et pro pleniori robur solidiorenq̃ firmitatem perpetuis futuris temporibus obtineant Magistri Sociem zforeq̃ Notariis publicis requirimus in hijs scriptis quatenus hunc statutorum et ordinatio-num libellum Sigilli nostri appensione munitum et roboratum sig-no et subscriptione sua ceu decretum a nobis profectum testetur et subscribat.

Jo. Roffensis

evangelists with scrolls bearing inscriptions from the Scriptures which indicate the meaning of the scenes; these texts are nearly all taken from the Vulgate, the Latin Bible of the Middle Ages, and their use in the decorative scheme of the windows is like that of the psalm antiphons in the divine office, with which they are often identical.

Typological composition of this kind was common in the Middle Ages and is found in many of the popular *Biblia pauperum* (literally, 'Bibles for poor people'; they were series of pictures illustrating the main biblical events) but rarely had it been exemplified on such a grandiose scale and with such splendid expression. We know who drew up this particular scheme from a memorandum of 30 November 1515 which states that the work was to be done 'in such forme and condition as my Lord of Winchester shal devise and commande to be doone'.[2] This refers to Richard Foxe, graduate of Oxford and Louvain, friend of Henry VII in exile and founder of Corpus Christi College, Oxford. He also had strong Cambridge connections and was Master of Pembroke from 1507-1519 and Chancellor of the University. He had been Bishop of Winchester since 1501; associated with him was Robert Hacomblen, the devout and deeply orthodox Provost of King's from 1509 to 1528. The artists and glaziers who worked at King's for over thirty years to complete this magnificent task followed the style of the Renaissance as developed in northern Europe; they were an international group and we know the names of some of them, Germans, Dutchmen, Flemings and some Englishmen. There are close parallels to the windows at Antwerp, Brussels and Rouen, exhibiting the same striving after a naturalistic effect and the same love of rich, varied colours and lush design. What makes the windows at King's so effective is in part the contrast between the sinuous style of the glass, full of warmth and movement, and the austere vertical lines of the Perpendicular tracery.

The east window, over the high altar, departs from the general plan of Old Testament *type* and New Testament *antitype*. It portrays the climax of Christ's passion in six scenes, the *Ecce homo*, Pilate washing his hands and Christ carrying the cross in the lower scenes, and, above, Christ nailed to the cross, the death of Christ and the descent from the cross. These scenes dominate the chapel, forming the focal point of the whole composition. Not only is there an ironic contrast between Pilate, portrayed as a Renaissance prince on a magnificent throne, and Christ above, reigning from the wood of the cross; but the redemptive death of the Saviour gives its meaning to the whole scheme of salvation portrayed in the two converging series on north and south. It is particularly significant that the series begins and ends with Mary; in the first window of the northern side her Immaculate Conception is depicted, as is usual in the Middle Ages, by the scene of the meeting of Joachim and Anna at the Golden Gate of the Temple, and her Assumption and Coronation terminate the series in the last window on the southern side. This is a profoundly Catholic understanding of the role of Mary in the history of salvation as the one who more than any other receives the grace of God and as the epitome of redeemed human nature. These doctrines were not defined as a part of the Church's traditional understanding of the gospel until many centuries later (the Immaculate Conception by Pius IX in 1854 and the Assumption by Pius XII in 1950), but here, long before the dogmatic definitions, they are clearly proclaimed as part of the Church's faith. This proclamation, moreover, takes place in a teaching context, in a chapel built for some of the teachers and students of the University of Cambridge.

The windows of King's are sometimes described as representing the end of a long tradition. Mr Wayment, in his great work on their iconography, talks of 'a doomed medieval formula'.[3] On this two comments need to be made. Firstly, that the place given to Mary in the scheme of redemption in the windows of King's corresponds to the view that the Second Vatican Council expresses in its chapter on Our Lady:[4] Mariology is a part of Christology, but not a part which can be dispensed with.

Secondly, the constant reference of the Old and New Testament to each other is a traditional Christian view of the Bible which neither began nor ended with the Middle Ages. Perhaps the best modern expression of the same view is the new lectionary of the Roman Church, produced in 1969 as a result of the liturgical reforms of the Second Vatican Council. In a carefully structured two-year cycle, readings from the Old and New Testament are now meaningfully related to each other in the daily liturgy.

It is ironical that the east window of the chapel was being put into place at the very time when the Royal Supremacy was being imposed on the Church in England. The contrast between Christ and Pilate takes on a poignant actuality when it is considered that these figures may well have been made in the years which saw the imprisonment and execution of St John Fisher and St Thomas More.[5] By happy chance, the windows of King's chapel escaped the destruction of the ensuing centuries; today their beauty enchants countless visitors whether it is the summer sun which shines through them to fill the chapel with dappled colours or the even light of an East Anglian winter which enhances their tonality of silver and blue. Their message is always the same, that the Scriptures are fully understood only in reference to Christ and to the community which continues his work. Here too there is an irony of history, for it was in the very years that the Catholic faculty of theology in Cambridge was suppressed that its teaching was transmuted into such incomparable form and colour for all the world to see.

With such cultural achievements, it is difficult to think of men like Fisher as living in 'the late Middle Ages'. In so many ways modern scholarship had arrived, and it is also important to stress the influence of the new Cambridge on the wider world. The episcopate during the reign of Henry VIII included several Cambridge men; some, like Latimer, were later actively Protestant but others could be described as typical Catholic bishops of their epoch, although they gave way to the king when the time of testing came. Such was Stephen Gardiner (1483–1555), a Fellow and Master of Trinity Hall and Doctor of both Civil and Canon Law; as Bishop of Winchester he supported Henry over the divorce issue but favoured the generally Catholic tone of Henry's Six Articles and returned to influence under Mary. He also maintained scholarly interests, corresponding with John Cheke on Greek pronunciation, and he was a not inappropriate Chancellor of the University from 1540 to 1547 and again from 1553 to 1555. Nicholas West, Bishop of Ely until 1533, had been a Fellow of King's from 1483 to 1498, and in the Reformation years he was

Chaplain to Queen Catherine of Aragon and a leading opponent of the Divorce. Erasmus's Cambridge friends included Foxe and Ruthall, respectively Bishops of Winchester and Durham, and the other leading ecclesiastics from the environment of Catholic

17. St Edward's Church and King's College Chapel. This view from the Guildhall shows two of Cambridge's landmarks rising above the roofs of the old town. The church of St Edward King and Martyr is dedicated to a little known West Saxon saint; its tower dates from the thirteenth century and its simplicity contrasts with the grandeur of King's College Chapel, begun on a colossal scale by Henry VI in 1446 and only finished under Henry VIII in 1515. This view shows how medieval buildings arose out of the crowded tenements of the town; the lawns and broad vistas are a later embellishment of Cambridge. (Photograph by Alan Rooke)

reform were, of course, Fisher of Rochester and Tunstall of Durham.

Cuthbert Tunstall was a graduate of King's Hall and he became Bishop of London (1520–1529) and Durham (1529–1559). On his translation, he gave the University Library a notable collection of Greek works, including an *editio princeps* of Homer and an Aristotle; he also gave the first English arithmetic book and, a great treasure, a copy of the Complutensian Polyglot Bible, a critical edition of the Bible with text and translations in parallel columns published in Spain in 1521. Tunstall could not be described as a Confessor of the Catholic faith, still less as a martyr. Though loyal to most aspects of the Catholic teaching, he believed in passive obedience to the civil power and so, like Gardiner, he accepted Henry's creation, a Catholic Church in an independent English framework—the Church of the Six Articles. But in later life he was a firm opponent of Edwardian radical protestantism and was deprived of his bishopric in 1552. He was restored by Mary in 1554 and again deprived by Elizabeth for refusing the oath of supremacy. So perhaps men like these are not wholly out of place in a study of the Catholic traditions of Cambridge. Other compromisers, who accepted the divorce but wished to maintain a Catholic framework, included men like John Clerk, Bishop of Bath and Wells, and Robert Aldrich, Bishop of Carlisle (King's). Indeed one could describe the Henrician Catholic Church as the last gasp of Cambridge Catholic reform, for the strongest support for the Six Articles came from these Cambridge-educated bishops.

Apart from the bench of bishops, the Catholic reformers were strong in precisely those religious orders never seriously criticised for laxity or worldliness. The superb Bridgettine house of Syon comprised some sixty nuns, directed by twenty-five brethren as chaplains. In 1500 these included at least six Cambridge Fellows and many graduates. One member was the Welshman, Richard Whitford, a Fellow of Queens' from 1495 to 1504. He travelled with Lord Mountjoy, another Queens' man, and the two met Erasmus in Paris. In 1504 Whitford became chaplain to Bishop Foxe but in 1507 he entered Syon, where he translated many devotional works including the *Imitation of Christ* and the mystical writings of Walter Hilton; he also composed the *Jesus Psalter,* so popular in English Catholic piety until the nineteenth century. Also at Syon was Richard Reynolds, a friend of Whitford and of Thomas More, who was a Fellow of Corpus during Erasmus's stay in Cambridge. Among the monasteries faithful to the highest traditions of their order the London Carthusian house, or Charterhouse, was preeminent, and in 1531 the new prior was a Cambridge graduate, John Houghton. His monks included a Christ's man, William Exmew, described as a man of exceptional ability and a Greek scholar, while other Cambridge Carthusians of lesser note were John Rochester and Sebastian Newdigate.

There was thus a fair prospect in the twenties of the sixteenth century that a generation of men educated in Fisher's Cambridge would be able to carry out a truly Catholic reform of the English Church, bishops and other graduates reforming the parishes, and religious, like the Carthusians and Bridgettines, providing the model for a renewed monasticism. From this point of view, it would have seemed likely that Cambridge was beginning a long period of pre-eminence as the spiritual and intellectual heart of a renewed and reformed Catholic Britain. The outcome was to prove very different.

Notes and References to Chapter 3

1. H. C. Porter, ed., *Erasmus and Cambridge* (Toronto, 1963); and his *Reformation and reaction in Tudor Cambridge* (Cambridge, 1958); Jean Simon, *Education and Society in Tudor England* (Cambridge, 1979: paperback edition); E. E. Reynolds, *Saint John Fisher* (London 1955); D. Knowles, *The Religious Orders in England*, iii. *The Tudor Age* (Cambridge, 1959); and his *Saints and Scholars* (Cambridge, 1963), pp. 175–178.
2. H. Wayment, *The Windows of King's College Chapel Cambridge: Corpus Vitrearum Medii Aevi, Great Britain Supplementary Volume I* (London, British Academy, 1972), p. 2.
3. *Ibidem,* p. 8.
4. Dogmatic Constitution *Lumen Gentium*, 21 November 1964 (CTS Do 349), Chapter 8.
5. Cf. H. Wayment, *The Windows of King's College Chapel Cambridge.* pp. 82–83.

four:

Cambridge and the Reformation

It is only hindsight which makes us view the first decades of the sixteenth century solely as a background to, or a preparation for, the Protestant Reformation. At the time circumstances seemed favourable to the Catholic reformers, and they might indeed have succeeded had political events not intervened. But Protestantism was in existence at Cambridge from very early times; as Dr H. C. Porter has pointed out, many later Protestant leaders commenced Bachelor between about 1510 and 1520, the years which saw Erasmus at work and a general return to scriptural sources. Such were Cranmer of Jesus, Latimer of Clare and a dozen of lesser celebrity. Latimer was a Fellow of Clare from 1506 to 1530, under the very conservative Master, Edmund Natures; by the early fifteen-twenties he was drawing close to two other reformers, Thomas Bilney of Trinity Hall and Robert Barnes of the Augustinian friars. All three institutions used St Edward's as their parish church and it therefore became the centre of Lutheran-inclined preaching in Cambridge, just as the nearby *White Horse Tavern* was a centre for meeting and discussion for the early Reformers.

The Cambridge Reformers emerged from the colleges but also from the religious houses, Barnes's Austin friars and Barnwell under its prior, Thomas Rawlyn. At first they were rigorously suppressed; Bilney was burnt as a heretic at Norwich in 1531 and became the first Protestant martyr of Cambridge, the first of twenty-five. Both Latimer and Barnes would die similar deaths in later years. But, after the divorce controversy, the new religion found state support and it soon came to dominate the colleges. In 1530 the Bishop of Norwich wrote that he hears of Gonville Hall that 'no clerk that hath come out lately of it but savoureth of the frying pan, though he speak never so holily';[1] soon such men would have the upper hand in both Church and State. Henry VIII had at first followed the family tradition of sympathy towards the Catholic reformers, but now they were the first to perish. Between 1535 and 1544 there were at least forty Catholic martyrs and of these nine or ten were Cambridge men. St John Houghton, Prior of the London Charterhouse, was the Catholic proto-martyr of the Reformation; he was a B.A., B.D., and LL.B. of Cambridge and was executed at Tyburn on 4 May 1535. In all no less than eighteen of the martyrs were Carthusians, men like William Exmew, Sebastian Newdigate and John Rochester. St Richard Reynolds, a Bridgettine from Syon Abbey, perished on the same day as Houghton, although Whitford was given refuge by his old pupil, Lord Mountjoy. Fisher was executed on 22 June 1535, after having been made a Cardinal by Pope Paul III; his death marks the end of the hopes of Catholic reform in England as a whole no less than in Cambridge. Among the others who resisted Henry's supremacy were Richard Fetherston, a secular priest, and German Gardiner, secretary to Bishop Stephen Gardiner.

Piece by piece the old Cambridge died. The Corpus Christi procession ended in 1535 and the religious houses were all suppressed between 1536 and 1538. Ely was the greatest of these with estates worth nearly £1,100 a year, but there were many smaller houses, such as Barnwell with its £350 income; and it should not be thought that these institutions were moribund. Both the Dominican and Franciscan houses had between twenty and thirty friars on dissolution and they had produced vigorous supporters both of Protestant Reform and of Catholic tradition. In its last years Greyfriars held at the same time men of strong orthodoxy, who would later become Observants, and progressive Protestants like Bartholomew Traherne; but in 1538 the whole friary was merely swept away along with its counterparts from the other orders.

The disappearance of the abbeys was especially unfortunate in these eastern counties as, whatever the spiritual effects, their painstaking monastic supervision of fen drainage was now at an end. Here the Dissolution was a catastrophe from which no recovery was possible until the sixteen-twenties. The transfer of lands chiefly benefited families who had built up their fortunes as gentry, men like Lord North who headed the Court of Augmentations (that is, 'augmentations of the royal income from monastic wealth'), or the Stywards of Ely, descended from the last prior of Ely, who became the first dean of the secular Cathedral Chapter. Middle class families also endeavoured to establish themselves, as did Hobson, the carrier, with the Anglesey estates derived from the former abbey of Augustinian canons, or the Butlers with the Barnwell lands, both in the seventeenth century. It must be admitted that in so many ways the Reformation was a disaster for the area, even if the religious aspects of the crisis are left out of consideration. Schools especially suffered from the destruction of the chantries in the fifteen-forties, while the initial effect on the University Library was one of 'terrible destruction and neglect'. This was not the result of deliberate vandalism but of a belief that the medieval volumes were now irrelevant, relics of a world that had passed away. Certainly there was recovery in the later years of Elizabeth, symbolised for example by the acquisition of the *Codex Bezae* in 1581,[2] but the middle decades of the century were disastrous. Material ruin also overtook the old monastic fabrics; Barnwell was quite swept away. Thorney was plundered to provide stone for Trinity and Corpus. Iconoclasm was also severe; the shrines of St Etheldreda and her sister at Ely were destroyed in 1541 and a renewed policy of iconoclasm was ordered from above in the fifteen-forties. In 1541 Bishop Goodrich ordered his clergy in the diocese of Ely 'to see that all images, relics, table-monuments of miracles, shrines. etc., be so totally demolished and obliterated with all speed and diligence that no remains or memory might be found of them for the future.'[3] Of course this was not immediately accomplished and much remained to be destroyed in later waves of Puritan zeal, but eventually the churches of the area lost what must have been a splendid heritage of stained glass, sculpture, vestments and wall-paintings. College chapels were not exempt as is shown by the case of St John's, where the memorial plaque of the last Catholic Master was defaced at about this time; service books and vestments were systematically destroyed.

If the university suffered in material terms, it also suffered as an educational institution. It lost books; monasteries no longer existed to send monk-students and various 'relics of popery', like the University Chaplaincy, were abolished in 1570. Although these gaps would soon be made good, the initial effects were clear. It was Latimer himself who wrote in 1550, 'It would pity a man's heart to hear that I hear of the state of Cambridge ... it will come to pass that we shall have nothing but a little English divinity, that will bring the realm into a very barbarousness and utter decay of learning. . . . There be none now but great men's sons in colleges and their fathers look not to have them preachers.'[4] Not all was loss; the monastic college of Buckingham perished, as did the monasteries which had supported it, like Walden in Essex. This now went to the profit of Lord Audley, like North an archetypal Tudor 'new man', but he endowed a new college in 1542 in the buildings of Buckingham College and called it Magdalene. In 1546 Trinity College came into being, a magnificent royal foundation, richly endowed with the properties of some twenty-four monasteries, and a sign that the crown favoured the universities and that they would not go the way of the other religious foundations which had recently disappeared. But even here there was loss; the old colleges of King's Hall and Michaelhouse were dissolved and their endowments given to Trinity, which was built on the site of several other small halls and hostels, as well as on what remained of Milne Street.

Protestantism spread rapidly, not least because of the vested interests created by the crown's distribution of monastic spoils. But it went deeper than this. It has been argued that the incidence of clerical marriage is a good index of Protestant sentiment, since it indicates not only how many clergy in an area were prepared to accept the new order, but also how many patrons were prepared to let them marry. In the diocese of London one third of the clergy were married by the time of Edward VI, making it as Protestant as Lancashire, with one twentieth of married clergy, was Catholic. After London, the counties of Essex, Norfolk and Suffolk were the most Protestant with one quarter of the clergy married, followed by Cambridgeshire with one fifth. This argues for rapid Protestant success at all levels of society, a success which drew, no doubt, on local Lollard and anti-clerical traditions.

In the university, Protestant advances were especially marked during the chancellorships of Somerset and Northumberland (1547–1553), but this was followed by the reign of Mary Tudor and the return of Gardiner (1553–1555). There was a general exodus of Reformers; of the 470 or so who went into exile under Mary, about ninety were or had been Cambridge men. Of those who remained, some were put to death for their religious beliefs; Ridley and Latimer were burnt at Oxford in 1555; Cranmer in 1556. John Hullier, Vicar of Babraham and formerly scholar of King's, was executed on Jesus Green in 1556, the only execution for heresy at Cambridge during Mary's reign.

But the supporters of the old ways were still strong enough in Cambridge to ensure an easy triumph for Gardiner and his successor as Chancellor of the University, Cardinal Pole. In 1554 Gardiner wrote to all the heads of houses, instructing them to contribute to the cost of a new processional cross to replace the medieval masterpiece sold in 1548 for £92. 18s. He explained that he had instructed the Vice-Chancellor 'to provyde a semely crosse of silver, for to be used in your processions, as hathe been among you in tymes past, and is through Christendom at this day observed.'[5] Since the new one cost £30. 0s. 8d. it must have been considerably less splendid but it was an affirmation of the Catholic character of the university and of the importance of its religious ceremonies. This was to be accompanied in the future by an explicit profession of the Catholic faith on the part of all those voting in university business or receiving a degree. As the result of a letter from Gardiner to the Vice-Chancellor in 1555 four Cambridge doctors drew up fifteen articles of faith;[6] they upheld those areas of the Catholic faith recently controverted by the Reformers, such as the reality of merit, the sacrificial character of the mass, the indissoluble nature of Christian marriage, purgatory, the validity of prayers for the dead, the holiness of religious vows, the visible nature of Christ's Church and its immunity from error in matters of faith.[7]

72

The new order was enforced by a group of Masters of varying degrees of conviction. Some, like Andrew Perne who was Master of Peterhouse from 1554 to 1589, were proverbial turncoats; when he put up a weathercock with his initials 'A.P.', they were said to stand for 'A Papist' or 'A Protestant' according to the direction of the wind: others however were more consistent. There was John Caius (1510–1573), a leading physician, who had been at Gonville Hall and refounded it as Gonville and Caius College in 1557. He was Master from 1559 to 1573 and, although he was for years a physician to Queen Elizabeth, he was dismissed from attendance in 1568 because he was a Catholic. There was George Bullock of St John's who became Master in 1554 and Lady Margaret Professor of Divinity in 1556. He was deprived of the posts for recusancy in 1559 and spent much of his life, a loyal Catholic, in Antwerp. King's Hall produced Edmund Cosin, one of the first Fellows of Trinity in 1546, Master of St Catharine's and Vice-Chancellor in 1558. He, as a Catholic, resigned all his offices in 1560 and from 1564 he retired to the protection of Dr Caius's college, but in 1564 he too fled abroad.

This general picture of scholarship and Catholic loyalty is confirmed by the Master of Pembroke, John Young. Like Bullock, he had been a Fellow of St John's and, like Cosin, one of the first Trinity Fellows. In 1554 he obtained his position as Master, served as Vice-Chancellor and became Regius Professor of Divinity, but on the accession of Elizabeth he was deprived and imprisoned for refusing the new oaths. Finally, among this 'hard core', we should count the secular priest, Philip Baker, Provost of King's in 1558 who, in 1563, was accused of sheltering the Dominican Thomas Heskins. Just as Caius preserved the medieval vestments of Gonville Hall until they were found and destroyed in 1573, so Baker refused to destroy his 'deal of popish stuff' which he kept in a 'secret corner'.[8] In 1569 he lost his Provostship and fled to Louvain to avoid an episcopal visitation.

It was such men who were to support the visitation of the university carried out by the authority of Cardinal Pole in January and February 1557. The visitors were headed by Cuthbert Scot, Bishop of Chester and Master of Christ's. With him were Thomas Watson, Bishop-elect of Lincoln, a former Master of St John's who was to die in prison under Queen Elizabeth; John Christopherson, Master of Trinity, soon to be Bishop of Chichester, who also died in prison for the Catholic faith; Henry Cole, Provost of Eton, and Nicholas Ormanetto, an Italian priest, who was a Datary, that is, a member of the papal chancery.

The visitation began with considerable ceremony on 11 January when the whole university, in academic dress, processed behind its new cross from Great St Mary's to Trinity Great Gate where the visitors were waiting for them. There was a Latin speech from the university orator, after which all went in procession to King's College Chapel where the Votive Mass of the Holy Spirit was celebrated; then, another procession to Great St Mary's for the formal reading of the visitors' commission and a sermon.[9]

The event in connection with this official visitation of the university which has been remembered by posterity is the gruesome ceremony which took place in the Market Place on 6 February when the remains of two heretics, Martin Bucer and Paul Fagius, which had been dug up, were burnt, together with a cart load of heretical books.[10] It was a symbolic purification of what was intended to be henceforth a Catholic university, but the work of the visitors was not limited to symbolic acts. All the foundation documents and charters of the university and colleges were called for and read so that it could be ascertained whether they were being observed. All the officers of the university were examined, often one by one, to test their orthodoxy, and then all the doctors and readers, who were also questioned about the authors they read and how they lectured and held disputations. Every aspect of the university's life was enquired into.

There was a new and business-like approach about the proceedings which is characteristic of the Counter-Reformation. Gone was the rather lax approach of late medieval Cambridge. When the Provost of King's protested that he was answerable to the Pope alone and to no other visitors, the ground of his protest was accepted but held not to apply since the authority of Cardinal Pole was equivalent to that of the Pope; as Legate *a latere* in England the Cardinal was an *alter ego* of the Pope,[11] and the visitors were acting on the Cardinal's authority. Recourse could no longer be had to a thicket of immunities and dispensations so as to prevent anything effective ever being done. King's was the first of the colleges to be visited; the proceedings began with mass in the chapel at seven in the morning, after which a roll call of the members took place, and then the pyx where the Blessed Sacrament was kept and the sacristy were inspected to see that everything was in order. After that the Provost and Vice-Provost and the other members of the college were examined until four o'clock.

One by one all the colleges were thus examined and shortcomings were noted. At Corpus Christi, for instance, there was no crucifix or holy water in the chapel and the holy oils were not under lock and key; also, the Fellows appeared to be ignorant of the duties laid on them by their statutes. Other kinds of shortcomings were also dealt with when, for example, someone was committed to prison 'for suffrynge scholars to play at cardes in his howse'.[12]

On 8 February there was a Blessed Sacrament procession; it was not the liturgical period for such a procession but this one was obviously meant to reaffirm the corporate devotion of the university to a central tenet of the Catholic faith. Bishop Scot carried the Blessed Sacrament but the university had presumably lost its vestments, since the cope he wore came from Christ's and the monstrance had to be borrowed from Gonville Hall. The procession started at Trinity, went up to the Round Church and then to Great St Mary's by Petty Cury. It was not the right time of year for an outdoor procession either and all the gowns of the university men got terribly muddy; there was also a mishap with the canopy over the Blessed Sacrament which was set alight by one of the torches. Six days later Bishop Scot held ordinations in Christ's College chapel and gave the tonsure, which marked entry into the clerical state, to all the scholars of Trinity and St John's and some others, about two hundred in number.[13]

The visitation ended on 17 February and the visitors worked hard afterwards for, on 15 May 1557, new statutes for the university and the colleges of Cambridge were delivered to the Vice-Chancellor and to the Heads of Houses. Cardinal Pole's statutes were in force for a short time only, since they were rescinded at the beginning of Elizabeth's reign, but they are of interest in indicating the kind of university that the Counter-Reformation would have produced. It was to be severely Catholic; anyone attacking the authority of the Church in speech or writing, anyone reading, possessing, or selling heretical books, anyone ridiculing the ministers or ceremonies of the Church, was to be excluded from his college or hall at the first offence, and from the university at the second.[14]

Mass was to be celebrated in every college daily between five and six in the morning and everyone was to attend. Each college was to provide up to three priests for hearing confessions and also to make sure that there was a priest to bring communion to the sick and to visit them regularly. In addition to making their Easter duties all members of the colleges, including the servants, were to go to confession and communion at the following feasts: Pentecost, the Assumption, All Saints, Christmas and on the patronal feast of the college.[15] There were in addition a considerable number of rubrical injunctions, of the type soon to be enjoined on the whole Church by the Tridentine Missal of Pius V, about when those attending mass and the office should sit, kneel or stand and how they were to behave in processions. Perhaps behaviour was so bad that explicit rules were necessary, since one of them was that no one should blow his nose on his surplice.[16]

But the prospects of a truly Catholic reform in Cambridge depended on national events; the early death of Mary led to the accession of Elizabeth and a Protestant settlement in Church and university. It would be too simple to talk of what followed as a purge, especially as Caius survived in his college until 1573, and the speed of the change-over in some colleges was accelerated by the early deaths of Marian Masters through natural causes; but by the fifteen-sixties religious attitudes were hardening and the St Bartholomew's Massacre led to new anti-Catholic measures. Moreover the radicals were clearly in the ascendant; in 1565 a Corpus man called for the destruction of all superstitious painted glass in the university. The rood loft of Great St Mary's lost its crucifix in 1562 and the whole loft went in 1569. This was representative of what was happening throughout the university.

From the fifteen-sixties Cambridge was beginning to return to national pre-eminence, but as a Puritan centre. Men like Thomas

Cartwright were national leaders of the Puritan cause, while the ultra-Protestant loyalty of the town was cemented by 'lectureships' in churches like St Clement's and Holy Trinity. In the fifteen-eighties Puritan 'seminaries' appeared at Emmanuel and Sidney Sussex, and Christ's acquired a very low church atmosphere. But the Catholics had not entirely left. Caius survived until 1573 and during that decade there were dons like Humphrey Cartwright of Christ's (later a Jesuit) and Richard Willoughby of Corpus, soon to become a Catholic convert. A more significant figure was Thomas Heskins (Clare; M.A. 1540), Chancellor of Salisbury under Mary, who went into exile after Elizabeth's accession. He joined the Dominicans in the Low Countries and anticipated later seminary priests in carrying out under-cover work in England, being sheltered by the Provost of King's. He also published controversial writings on the Eucharist, so that in many ways he bridged the gap between the Catholic reformers of Fisher's age and the heroic missionaries of the final decades of the sixteenth century.

It is possible to see the history of Catholic Cambridge at this point as an afterglow of medievalism and to assume that nothing is to be found for our subject between 1570 and the 'Second Spring'. What should prevent such an attitude is the silent witness of the Cambridge men put to death as Catholics between 1581 and 1681 (see Appendix I, pp. 140–4). Of the thirty-four or so who are known to have been executed or who died in prison, nine perished during the Henrician Reformation; fifteen followed between 1581 and 1612, and then ten more between 1641 and 1681.

The Jesuits and seminary priests began to arrive in England in 1574 and they fully realised the importance of converting the influential, those who, in a hierarchical society, could do much to lead others to Catholicism. In 1581 Persons himself wrote of the significance of Cambridge: 'I have at length insinuated a certain priest into the very university under the guise of a scholar or gentleman commoner and procured him help from a place not far from the city.'[17] His work bore fruit although it is difficult to give an exact picture of what had perforce to be an underground movement; however in the case of Caius College a corner of the veil can be lifted. This college seems to have been especially congenial to Catholics under Caius's successor, Dr Legge, who was Master for more than thirty years and whose sympathies lay with the old religion. J. Venn has collected evidence of a considerable number of Caius men who either became priests abroad after leaving or who are known as recusants.[18] Thus Richard Holtby, who came up in 1573, went on to become in time Superior of the English Jesuits. Robert Sayer, who was admitted to Caius in 1576, became a Benedictine monk at Monte Cassino. Christopher Walpole, the younger brother of St Henry Walpole, was at Caius from 1587 to 1590 and entered the Society of Jesus at Rome in 1592; and there were several more. Venn lists fourteen Catholic laymen, known recusants, who entered Caius College between 1564 and 1608; for the period 1570–98 the entries include six Caius men who are known to have become Jesuits later and eleven others who are recorded as having been subsequently ordained abroad.[19] This is a considerable number and it comes from one college only. It gives us some idea of the challenge which the Counter-Reformation was able to make to the Elizabethan religious settlement.

The wave of executions after 1581 shows the government's deep concern, bordering on panic, at the success of the seminary priests in gaining converts. The martyrs under Elizabeth and James I included Jesuits like St Henry Walpole and seminary priests like Blessed Everard Hanse and John Nutter. But there were also laymen, like St Philip Howard, Earl of Arundel, who had been a member of the Established Church when he was at Cambridge and who was later converted to Catholicism. He was condemned to death for treason in 1589 but was not executed and died in the Tower in 1595.

The outbreak of war with Spain in 1584 and the Armada in 1588 led to special tension; no less than seven Cambridge Catholics perished between 1584 and 1588. In such an atmosphere the government relaxed its scruples about applying capital punishment to lay Catholics below noble rank. In 1584 Wales acquired one of its first post-Reformation martyrs in St Richard Gwyn who had been at St John's College; he was hanged, drawn and quartered at Wrexham for 'persuading to popery' and was unusual among the martyrs in being a layman, a schoolmaster and the father of a large family. Another layman with strong Cambridgeshire links was St John Rigby from Lancashire who became in 1595 the steward of Sir Edmund Huddleston of Sawston Hall, a place of which we shall have much to say. Rigby was condemned for being reconciled to the Church and, at Southwark in 1600, he suffered the same appalling death as Richard Gwyn.

In many cases the lives of these martyrs contain only fleeting references to Cambridge, but in evaluating this we should remember the wider context. By the early seventeenth century it was much less likely that the son of a Catholic squire would attend Cambridge University. If it is recorded of one of these martyrs that he had been here as an undergraduate, this suggests that he was converted to Catholicism, either at Cambridge or afterwards, and this is a remarkable fact. It throws new light on the Reformed Cambridge of the Jacobean period and indicates that, although the religion of the recusants was rooted in the medieval Church, it was also a vibrant and expanding religion, with new ideas and devotions which appealed to wholly new categories in society.

It is often difficult to provide exact dates for conversions but two examples of early seventeenth century converts are provided by the martyrs, St Alban Roe and St Henry Morse. Roe, a Suffolk man, left Cambridge for Douai and became a Benedictine before 1612. He returned to England between about 1615 and 1623; after capture and a long imprisonment he was condemned for being a priest and executed in 1642, just as the protection of Charles I was being removed from his recusant subjects. Morse's career was similar but we can supply the name of his college. He was another Suffolk man and entered Corpus Christi before 1620. Soon afterwards he was a student at Douai and by 1625 he was a Jesuit. He too perished during the period of Puritan domination in 1645. Among the other martyrs, the Venerable Henry Heath was also converted about 1620, after being at Corpus, while Blessed Hugh Green was a Peterhouse undergraduate before being received in about 1610. Obviously, only a handful of Catholic converts went on to the priesthood and still fewer to actual martyrdom, so that these four converts between 1610 and 1620 can only be a small part of the whole story. This gives us a remarkable insight into the religious atmosphere of the university that also produced the radical Puritans associated with Emmanuel, Christ's and the parish of Holy Trinity, men like Sibbes, Perkins, Preston and Milton himself.

Another aspect of the religious life of the times is illustrated by William Alabaster (1567–1640), the poet, who was an undergraduate and later a Fellow of Trinity. He accompanied the Earl of Essex on his expedition to Cadiz in 1596 and declared himself a Catholic on his return. After some years living on the Continent he ran into trouble with the Inquisition, which ordered his imprisonment. After he was released he returned to his native land and to the Church of England, but his case is an interesting one of conversion to Catholicism in the last years of Elizabeth. We strongly suspect that if the sources were fuller many more instances could be found; as it is we have to rely on casual items of evidence, like that found in the will of Dr William Butler of Clare (1526–1618), an eminent physician who attended James I and his family. In his will, he disowns a brother who had turned papist, but of the brother himself little more can be discovered.

In the sixteen-twenties the Catholic religion was proving attractive for a number of new reasons. The Counter-Reformation made it appear a new and expanding force, not merely a survival fit only for the very old or the very conservative. Travel in Europe revealed to many Englishmen the magnificent works of art undertaken in the Catholic cause and these had great appeal in an age of fine aesthetic sensibility. 'Catholic art' could no longer imply a naive or even embarrassing depiction by a local artist in an English parish church. It evoked Mannerist painting or the sculpture and architecture of Bernini. In politics the victories of the Spanish and Imperial armies in Germany seemed to indicate that Protestantism was on the wane, while the courts of these countries offered a more impressive spectacle than the shambles of Jacobean court circles. Perhaps the most important factor was that the long religious wars had led by 1620 to a grave spiritual crisis; men were tempted to embrace atheism or Socinianism (which denied the divinity of Christ), or else they sought refuge in the absolute certainty offered by Calvinism or by the Catholic Church. By about 1630 these factors had resulted in the creation of a wholly new style at the English court. King Charles I was attempting to imitate the absolutism of his Hapsburg and Bourbon relatives while the English Church was seeking to satisfy the aesthetic and dogmatic longings of its educated laity. In this new Laudian atmosphere Cambridge played a significant part. Of the Laudian bishops, Richard Montagu had matriculated at King's in 1594; Lancelot Andrewes's Mastership of Pembroke had attracted his young relative, Matthew Wren, to that college, and it was Wren's Mastership of Peterhouse from 1625 that was to have important consequences for Catholicism and for the High Church party in the Church of England.

From about 1630 Peterhouse was the scene of a series of liturgical innovations which could be seen as tending towards Popery; these trends became more marked under Cosin, Wren's successor as Master, who was Vice-Chancellor in 1639. Peterhouse chapel acquired a crucifix, candles and an altar raised up on steps. This does not sound dramatic in terms of present-day Anglican practice but in the seventeenth century it was seen as at least halfway to Popery; and, despite the staunch Anglican loyalty of Wren and Cosin, others were directed towards Rome. The most outstanding convert was the poet Richard Crashaw (1613–1649), who matriculated at Pembroke in 1631 and migrated in 1636 to Peterhouse where he became a Fellow.

By the late sixteen-thirties Catholicism was clearly much more in the realm of permissible debate than it had been for almost a century. For example, Crashaw was influenced by an Anglican cleric of the same college, Robert Shelford, one of the first brave souls to deny that the Pope was Antichrist and to assert that the Roman Church was at least a part of the True Church. Such men were influenced by the devotional works of St Teresa of Avila, and Crashaw was also drawn towards catholic traditions by the example of Nicholas Ferrar, the Clare man who had established a religious community at Little Gidding in Huntingdonshire. Ferrar himself was a firm Protestant who did believe that the Pope was Antichrist and who asserted that if mass were celebrated in a room in his house he would tear the room down, but he read and translated works by Jesuits as well as the *Introduction to the Devout Life* by St Francis de Sales. His circle of Catholic friends included a martyr, the Venerable Robert Apreece (died 1644). Priests were frequent visitors at the house. As was to happen again in the nineteenth century, it proved difficult to establish a form of Protestant monasticism without encouraging its members to drift away into a wider Catholic movement. For many of Ferrar's circle, the peril was very real. As well as Crashaw, we know of Andrew Marvell, the poet and fervently anti-Papist pamphleteer of the Restoration years, who had been 'perverted' to the Catholic Church by Jesuits in 1633 while an undergraduate at Trinity; his father brought him back to the Established Church within a year or two. It seems as though Catholicism was just in the air in the sixteen-thirties, as it would be again in the eighteen-forties, although the earlier movement is by no means as celebrated.

Positive Catholic influences in the area were now allowed to regroup and to prepare for new expansion under Jesuit leadership. It was in 1633 that the Jesuit 'College of the Holy Apostles' was formed. The term college was used to describe a missionary area where a number of Jesuits worked, although they did not live together. In this case the 'College' covered the counties of Norfolk, Suffolk, Essex and Cambridge and its centres were at Chelmsford and the great house of Lord Petre in Essex. Petre gave the college a capital sum of £4,000 in ready money, plus a perpetual income of £250. There were usually sixteen priests attached to the college, including one or two at any given time in Cambridgeshire. The college's annual letters give a good idea of the fortunes of the new Catholic movement. By 1635 the letters are noting a new 'high' or 'ritualistic' movement within the Established Church itself which extended as far as attempts at instituting confession. In 1637 it was noted that a Cambridge M.A. had been received and in 1639 he was followed by the Fellow of an unspecified Cambridge college. The latter was deprived of his position, arrested and tried, whereupon he was ordered under heavy bail not to leave the country.

By the critical years of 1640–1642 Cambridge was in the difficult position of being a high or Anglo-Catholic centre in what was clearly the most vigorously Puritan area of England. In the events leading to the outbreak of the Civil War in 1642, the most important single factor was probably the widespread suspicion that the king was too sympathetic to Catholics, whether in Spain or in Ireland. The Irish revolt of 1641 made civil violence in England almost inevitable, and Cambridgeshire was bound to reflect the ensuing plots and rumours of wars. From 1638 the Bishop of Ely had been none other than Matthew Wren, late Master of Peterhouse, petitions against whom had been a major form of protest against Catholic influences in the government of Charles I. In an atmosphere of popular iconoclasm, these petitions attacked all forms of Popery; they asked Parliament to effect 'the removing of unwarranted orders and dignities, the steps unto Popery, the purging of the University, the banishing of Popish clergy' as well as 'the relieving of our distressed brethren abroad and fortifying ourselves at home.'

Soon preparations were made for defence and commissioners were appointed 'for disarming Popish recusants and other dangerous persons in the county of Cambridge'. Bishop Wren was regarded as dangerous, if not actively Popish. In 1642 a pamphlet, *Joyful News from the Isle of Ely,* told how the Bishop had been arrested as 'one of the greatest papists . . . in the whole kingdom'. When war broke out in August 'well-affected' (i.e. Parliamentarian) cavalry met near Cherry Hinton 'with an intent to search all papists' houses thereabouts, in which search they found but small store of arms and ammunition, at which they not a little wondered.'[20] Their surprise was caused by the current belief that Catholics were about to rise and massacre the Protestants.

The lack of evidence for Catholic plotting in no way diminished the virulent anti-popery of the area and there now began a wave of iconoclasm which completed the ruin begun under Henry VIII and Elizabeth. The chief villain was William Dowsing, who in the winter of 1643–1644 toured the area destroying everything that smacked of Popery; in the process he probably ruined some of the best vernacular art in British history. At Holy Trinity on Christmas Day 'we brake down eighty Popish pictures, and one of Christ and God the Father above.' In the Round Church there were fourteen such pictures, as well as 'divers idolatrous inscriptions'. Country parishes like Chesterton did not escape; here he destroyed fourteen crosses on the steeple, two on the porch and forty 'superstitious' pictures; he also ordered the destruction of fifty more pictures and the levelling of the altar steps. At Little St Mary's there were sixty pictures for destruction, including some of the popes, and one which, judging from Dowsing's bigoted description, must have portrayed God the Father seated on a throne, surveying the globe of the world.[21]

This last act of destruction has a particular significance as Little St Mary's was the church where Crashaw had worshipped. By this time it would have been clear to men such as Crashaw that the physical destruction of the contents of their churches was but one aspect of the wider ruin of the Anglican Church. To such men it would appear that Hooker and Laud had been wrong, that there was no *via media* but a simple choice between Rome and Geneva. The road to Rome was now followed by a number of Cambridge men, including Crashaw. He was received into the Catholic Church in about 1645 and soon afterwards found his way to Rome. Here he was visited by a former colleague, John Bargrave, who wrote in 1649 of this visit, 'There were there four revolters to the Roman Church that had been Fellows of Peterhouse with myself.' We cannot identify these four with certainty but other converts of this period can be named. Blessed Edward Coleman, executed in 1678, had been at Trinity until his conversion in mid-century. The Leicestershire Jesuit, Blessed Anthony Turner, was educated at Peterhouse and St John's before his conversion in the sixteen-forties; like Coleman he was later a casualty of the 'Popish Plot'. Christopher Banks, Fellow of Peterhouse, was converted to Catholicism by Fr John Heaton S.J. He was twenty-six at the time and was received into the Church on 4 July 1642; he lost no time in going to the English College, Rome, since he tells us that he sailed from Dover 'the next Sunday'. Banks was ordained in 1647 and went on to a long apostolate in Lancashire and Yorkshire until his death in 1678.[22] Another example of conversion at this time is provided by the controversialist, John Sergeant (1622–1707), who was at St John's College and, after his graduation in 1643, became secretary to the Anglican Bishop Morton; after the apparent collapse of the Church of England he became a Catholic in about 1645.

Some members of Catholic families are also recorded as being in Cambridge about this time; thus Thomas, Henry and Philip Howard were admitted fellow-commoners at St John's in July 1640.[23] They were not in Cambridge long, for by August 1641 they had been taken to Antwerp, out of reach of the Roundheads. Philip Howard later became a Dominican, the restorer of the English Province of the Friars Preachers, and was created Cardinal in 1675. Under the Commonwealth, Francis Throckmorton came to Cambridge in 1654 at the age of fourteen and stayed until 1658; he was head of the recusant Throckmortons of Coughton in Warwickshire and does not appear to have been a member of any college or to have matriculated. He resided in rented lodgings, studied privately and was attended by two menservants; his account book has survived and gives a detailed picture of the expenses of a young aristocrat at that period.[24]

In these years there was a double temptation to Rome. Royalist exiles wandering in France and Italy were exposed to a Catholic environment of peculiar intensity; for those who remained in England, there was the missionary activity of Jesuits and seminary priests who enjoyed remarkable freedom of action under Cromwell's rule. Of the 350 or so Catholic martyrs who were put to death in England and Wales between 1535 and 1681, only three perished between 1647 and 1660. In the area of the Jesuit 'College of the Holy Apostles' there were nineteen Fathers active in 1655, including one, Philip Compton, of Cambridgeshire. They continued to report successes; for instance, in 1650 they reported the conversion of a talented Cambridge scholar, who thus sacrificed any chance of academic advancement, a real sacrifice as he had hitherto been a highly respected preacher in the Protestant cause. Another convert was Jeremiah Hackluit, Cambridge M.A. and son of the Anglican minister of Stretham in Cambridgeshire; he served as a naval gunner in the war against the Dutch and was received in 1666 by Dr Leyburn, President of the English College at Douai.[25] There are other indications that, even in this heartland of Puritanism, conversions did occur. Thus John Huddleston, who became a Jesuit novice in 1655, recorded how his mother, who came from Wilbraham in Cambridgeshire, had taken him to Protestant services until her conversion in 1648. How many Anglicans were reconciled to the Catholic Church at this nadir in Anglican fortunes, between 1646 and 1651? Were there as many in the countryside as in the university? We just do not know, and it must be our constant regret that we cannot find out more about the means employed in missionary activity during these years of crisis.

In 1660 the Church of England was restored, with old Laudians like Wren and Cosin added to the episcopal bench. Charles II was even more sympathetic to Catholicism than his father had been; this was strongly suspected during his lifetime, although it was not proved until his deathbed reception into the Church by Dom John Huddleston, O.S.B. Alas for our story, Fr Huddleston was not a Cambridgeshire man and was related only distantly to the Sawston line of that family. The King's brother, the Duke of York, had declared himself a Catholic in 1672 and the politics of the next decade revolved around the probability of his succession to the crown and the likely consequences for English Protestantism. 'Exclusion' had a particular relevance to Cambridgeshire because of the presence there from about 1670 of the Earl of Dover, a Catholic and one of the closest friends of the Duke of York. He had bought Cheveley for no political reason but simply because magnates often occupied estates on the Suffolk-Cambridgeshire border because of the proximity to Newmarket and the races. However in a Catholic Britain Dover could be expected to wield enormous power and so his presence was seen as a threat and led to considerable resentment. He also appears to have kept a Carmelite as Chaplain so that there may have been two priests in the county by 1678, one at Sawston and one at Cheveley. In 1679 the Court felt obliged to eject justices whose anti-popery had led them to bitter criticism of the dynasty and in our area this included the powerful squires of Ditton and Impington. There were no executions in Cambridgeshire during the scare occasioned by the Popish Plot but three more Cambridge men were added to the list of martyrs in 1678–80 with the death of Edward Coleman, Anthony Turner, and William Howard, Viscount Stafford. Party violence was common in elections of this period, a trend which was exacerbated by the accession of James II in 1685.

The new king made it clear that Catholics would receive advancement and this must be adduced as one factor in the wave of conversions which occurred during his short reign. John Dryden the poet, who had been at Trinity from 1650 to 1654, became a Catholic c. 1685; Joshua Bassett of Caius was imposed by the king as the Catholic Master of Sidney Sussex College. Invoking his dispensing power, James II ordered the university to grant the degree of M.A. to a Benedictine, Dom Alban Francis, in spite of the tests which had been devised to exclude Catholics and Dissenters. The order was successfully resisted by the university; the delegation which pleaded the university's cause in the Court of High Commission in April 1687 included the great mathematician Isaac Newton, even though he held a fellowship at Trinity in virtue of a royal dispensation since he had doctrinal objections to taking Anglican orders.[26] It was characteristic of James's policy that it managed to unite in opposition all Protestants, even those who were outside the Anglican establishment.

At the same time James II was trying to secure a more amenable county community by purging obstreperous deputy-lieutenants and justices, a task made easier by the fact that Dover was now Lord-Lieutenant. A list of those 'that are right' included twenty Justices of the Peace, but twelve more were 'already put out, one to be put out'; it was potentially disastrous that the latter category included some of the county's greatest landowners. On the other hand, the king could not find enough converts to replace them and he certainly could not find men of similar social standing. In the sixteen-eighties the dioceses of Norwich, Lincoln and Ely had about four per cent of their population classified as Dissenters, but Catholics made up only 0·32%, 0·55% and 0·04% respectively. Only fourteen Catholics were recorded as resident in the diocese of Ely. Attempts were apparently made to rectify this: between 1684 and 1687 the number of Jesuits in the 'College of the Holy Apostles' rose from nine to twelve. Chapels were built in Norwich, Hertford and Bury St Edmunds, where there was also a school boarding eighteen youths of good families. For the Catholic missioners, Bury would long remain a kind of provincial capital. There is even a reference to a town chapel at Cambridge, but we have been unable to locate this more precisely. So, a Catholic establishment of sorts began to appear; by 1688 Cambridge had a Catholic mayor, 4% of the county Bench was Catholic and there was some limited infiltration into the colleges. It was a slow process but it would be fair to ask in comparison how long it had taken the Elizabethan regime to purge Catholic dons and Justices of the Peace. So far the opposition had been relatively limited because the heir presumptive to the crown was James's daughter, a Protestant. In June 1688 the queen bore a son who was baptized a Catholic and from then on revolution was virtually inevitable.

In Cambridgeshire the time of troubles was brief, chiefly because of the weakness of the Catholic party. Sir William Russell of Chippenham led the popular insurrection, appropriately since he was an anti-papist of long standing and a relative of Cromwell. Cheveley was attacked. James in general had little support; the long established Catholic families were appalled by his clumsy proselytism, Cardinal Howard being especially critical. By 1689 nothing remained of the high hopes of earlier years except for some new chapels and a few individuals whose conversion had been sincere. It was, for instance, in the inauspicious year of 1689 that one Clement Bolt of Caius went to Rome to become a priest.[27] But there could no longer be any hope that Laudian High Church policies could lead to any general shift to Rome; conversions now almost ceased, to be renewed in the very different circumstances of the nineteenth century. From 1688 it was clear that Catholicism could never become the religion of the State in England; it had to accept the status of a sect.

Notes and References to Chapter 4

1. *LP*, iv, part 3 (1876), p. 2876; no. 6385. Bishop Nix of Norwich [to the Duke of Norfolk]. Letter of 14 May, 1530.
2. In a way this was a dishonourable acquisition since the precious fifth century manuscript of the gospels had been looted from the Abbey of St Irenaeus at Lyons when the city was sacked by Huguenot soldiers in 1562. The Abbey was still in existence when Beza presented the codex to Cambridge, and the value of the manuscript was fully realised there since the Bishop of Clermont had produced it at the first session of the Council of Trent in 1548 as an early witness of the New Testament text and it had been collated while in Italy.
   See *Bezae Codex Cantabrigiensis,* edited by F. H. Scrivener (London, 1864), pp. vii–viii.
3. VCH, ii, p. 166.
4. VCH, iii, p. 176.

5. *The Letters of Stephen Gardiner,* edited by J. A. Muller (Cambridge, 1933), pp. 463–4. Letter dated 4 April, 1554.
6. *Ibidem,* pp. 475–6. Letter of 24 March, 1555.
7. J. Lamb, *A Collection of Letters, Statutes and Other Documents from the MS Library of Corp. Christ. Coll. illustrative of the History of the University of Cambridge during the Period of the Reformation* (London, 1838), pp. 172–5.
8. VCH, iii, p. 182.
9. J. Lamb, *Collection,* pp. 200–1.
10. *Ibidem,* p. 217.
11. *Ibidem,* pp. 201 and 212–3. See also R. H. Pogson, 'Cardinal Pole: Papal Legate to England in Mary Tudor's Reign' (unpublished Ph.D. dissertation, University of Cambridge, 1972), pp. 139–58, for an analysis of Pole's legatine powers.
12. J. Lamb, *Collection,* pp. 206–7.
13. *Ibidem,* pp. 218 and 222.
14. *Ibidem,* pp. 242–3.
15. *Ibidem,* p. 272.
16. *'Nemo tergat nasum superpellicio'; ibidem,* p. 272.
17. *Letters and Memorials of Father Robert Persons, S.J.,* edited by L. Hicks, i, CRS 39 (1942), pp. 98 (Latin text), 108 (translation). Letter of 21 October, 1581.
18. J. Venn, *Early Collegiate Life* (Cambridge, 1913); Chapter 7, 'An Elizabethan Episode in English History'.
19. *Ibidem,* pp. 89–102.
20. VCH, ii, p. 405.
21. J. G. Cheshire, 'William Dowsing's destructions in Cambridgeshire', *Cambridgeshire and Huntingdonshire Archaeological Society Transactions,* 3 (1914), pp.77–91.
22. *Responsa Scholarum of the English College Rome,* edited by A. Kenny, ii, CRS 55 (1963), pp. 475–6. Anstruther, ii, pp. 14–15.
23. BL, Add. 5850. f. 95. We are indebted to Dr Godfrey Anstruther, O.P. for this reference.
24. E. A. B. Barnard, *A Seventeenth Century Country Gentleman: Sir Francis Throckmorton 1640–80* (Cambridge, 1944), pp. 11-35.
25. *Responsa Scholarum,* ii, pp. 608-10.
26. See R. S. Westfall, *Never at Rest: a Biography of Isaac Newton,* (Cambridge, 1980), pp. 330-4.
27. Anstruther, iii, p. 19.

five:

Sawston Hall and Survival in Penal Times

The history of Cambridge Catholicism after the Revolution of 1688 must, of necessity, be the story of Catholics in the county as a whole, a story which is slender but not negligible. The main Catholic family in Cambridgeshire was the Huddlestons of Sawston about whom we have a great deal of evidence in the form of correspondence and other papers deposited in the Cambridgeshire Record Office. The Huddlestons are an old family, originally from Cumberland, who obtained the property at Sawston through marriage in the fifteenth century. John Huddleston was knighted for his services to Mary Tudor, who was at Sawston during the crisis at her accession; Northumberland pillaged and burnt the house on his way to Cambridge in 1553. As well as receiving a grant of stone from Cambridge Castle to rebuild Sawston, Sir John Huddleston was made a Privy Councillor to Queen Mary and also Vice-Chamberlain to King Philip of Spain; he married one of the Cottons of Landwade, a great family in the county, but most of his descendants differed from the general run of county society in that they had to go farther afield to find marriage partners of the same religion. We find the Huddlestons marrying into families from Catholic areas like Lancashire, Herefordshire, Monmouthshire and even Ireland. Sir Edmund Huddleston, the son of Sir John, married a Lancashire bride and was clearly of Catholic sympathies but he was sufficiently prosperous under the new order to build, between about 1557 and 1584, the splendid mansion that still stands today at Sawston. He was Sheriff of Essex in 1579–1580 and in 1588 and he died in 1606. He was probably a 'Church-papist', that is, an occasional conformist, but

his son was won over to firmer views by the Jesuit, Fr John
Gerard, who, between 1591 and 1594, lived and worked at
Braddocks, a house near Saffron Walden belonging to William
and Jane Wiseman. Jane was the daughter of Sir Edmund and
this is how Gerard describes the conversion of her brother, Henry
Huddleston.

> At this time I received into the Church my hostess's brother.
> He was the only son of a knight and he proved himself one
> of my most steadfast friends at all times. Later he married
> a cousin of the most illustrious Duke of Feria, and both are
> most devoted to our Fathers. They always have one of them
> in their house, sometimes two or three, quite regardless of the
> danger of the times.[1]

From that time the family at Sawston was what might be described
as a classic recusant gentry line. Henry died in 1657; his eldest
son and namesake was a Royalist colonel in the Civil War and
fought at Edgehill. The younger became a priest, served the
Hampshire district from 1642 to 1655, moving to the 'College of
the Holy Apostles' during his last years. Thereafter, the family
produced many priests and religious, especially nuns in the con-
vents of Paris, Bruges, Liege and Lisbon. Henry Huddleston (died
1713) had a sister who became a nun in Paris; his son Richard
was a typical East Anglian country squire, but his brother was a
priest, four sisters became nuns and the other sisters married into
recusant families: Gages and Fortescues. Richard's son was
another Richard (1715–1760), two of whose sisters became nuns,
but this was the last generation to produce so many vocations.
Between 1600 and 1760 the family had produced at least two
priests and seven nuns. There was in addition John Huddleston
or Dormer, the illegitimate son of Colonel Henry Huddleston's
brother. His mother became a convert to Catholicism about 1658,
whereupon his father sent him to St Omer. He was professed as
a Jesuit in 1673, to serve in Lincolnshire, and he earned some
celebrity when James II appointed him as a Royal Preacher at
the Court of St James. He escaped from England at the Revolution
but had returned by 1700, in which year he died in London.

The study of Catholicism among the gentry of Cambridgeshire

could be divided into two parts, the Huddlestons and the rest. Among the latter, the Paris's of Linton were recusants from the time of Ferdinand Paris in 1558 until the extinction of the family in the sixteen-sixties. Their house was a 'resort of suspected persons'; under William III the property passed to the Norfolk recusant family of Andrews, so that it continued to be owned by Catholics, but there was no active Catholic centre in Linton after 1670. Cheveley Hall belonged to the Catholic family of Jermyn, Earls of Dover, from 1671 to 1726. There was a Carmelite chaplain at Cheveley at the end of the century and a secular priest, John Lomax, in the seventeen-twenties, but afterwards the Catholic presence there came to an end. Any Catholic influence in the eastern part of the county derived from Bury St Edmunds, where there was a Jesuit school and mission in the sixteen-eighties.

There are occasional traces of Catholic individuals, but even the most hostile government was hard put to it to find them. In 1587 a Register of Papists for the county includes Henry Cooke of Milton, individuals at Hildersham and West Wratting, and six at Linton, members or servants of the Paris family. We find a number of Catholics registering lands between about 1715 and 1725 and at first sight Cambridgeshire seems to have acquired a Catholic gentry, with about ten land-owners, but further investigation shows that very few of these are local people. There are fenland farmers of moderate wealth, like Simon Hake of Chatteris and John Pitchford of Tydd St Giles, and some fenland parishes were dominated, surprisingly, by absentee papist land-owners, who lived in London, Essex, Lancashire and Bedfordshire – anywhere, it seems, except Cambridgeshire. One of the most substantial of these estates was at Whittlesey; it consisted of three manors, worth £1,900 a year and including some 18,000 acres of improveable fen, which belonged in the early eighteenth century to the Earl of Waldegrave, who was a Catholic. Other absentees included Mary Crane of London, owning lordships in half a dozen fen parishes, and Lady Petre, a member of the great Lancashire recusant family of Walmesley who had married one of the few Catholic peers in the eastern counties. But, of resident Catholics in 1715, only the obvious families have left a trace in the records, Lady Dover and the Huddlestons.

There is also a petty gentleman called Edward Wythie of Cambridge and a Mr Short; we only hear of the latter because during the scare caused by the Jacobite-rising of 1715 the Whig authorities seized the arms and horses of 'Mr Huddleston and Mr Short two Papists in this county'. In 1778 there is a reference to two leading Cambridgeshire Catholics, Ferdinand Huddleston (1737–1808) and Thomas Mitchell, Esquire. Mitchell is otherwise unknown.

So priests in the area could always count on the protection of at least one 'squire', sometimes two, and possibly on a gentleman or on a substantial fenland yeoman as well. From 1688 Cambridgeshire was included in the Midland District, the Bishops of which lived at Longbirch House at Brewood in Staffordshire from 1752 to 1804 and after that at Wolverhampton. Matters had settled down to a kind of secure lethargy. The number of Jesuits in the 'College of the Holy Apostles' was nineteen in 1655, ten in 1701 and twelve in 1773. There was normally one priest in Cambridgeshire, inevitably at Sawston. The historian of the Jesuit missions remarks of the eighteenth century that 'very scanty materials exist regarding the missions served by the Fathers of this College,'[2] but we can guess the identity of some of the Sawston priests. John Huddleston, who died in 1661, may have been based here, while in the sixteen-nineties a Jesuit called William Pennington was in residence. We have to rely on inventories referring vaguely to 'Mr Martin's chamber' in order to deduce the presence here in 1713 of John Martin, S.J., and from 1725 to 1776 the chaplain was John Champion, who emerges from the family correspondence as a combination of estate steward, messenger, legal adviser and spiritual guide. We see him reporting on the harvest and on negotiations about marriage settlements. Other Jesuit associates were responsible for educating the three sons of Richard Huddleston (who died in 1760), as is shown by a series of receipts dating from the late seventeen-forties. In 1757 the antiquary, William Cole of Milton, visited his friends the Huddlestons at Sawston and described the religious establishment thus:

The private Chapel is a gloomy Garret and no ways ornamented; it is quite out of the way by Design, and in Case of

93

any Confusion, the Tabernacle and Altar may easily be removed. Mr Champion, the Priest, has his Chamber close beyond it, he is a very worthy Jesuit and has lived in the Family these 30 years.[3]

Anti-papist searches were still a possibility, especially after the Jacobite scare of 1745–6. Champion served as Superior of the 'College' during the seventeen-forties. In 1773, in Champion's last years, European political divisions led to the suppression of the Jesuits. This accounts for the unprecedented appearance of Dominican chaplains at Sawston in the seventeen-eighties.

The rumour that the Jesuits were to be suppressed had caused much disturbance and hopes were expressed that the Pope would not succumb to the argument, 'If you release this man, you are no friend of Caesar's'; but such controversial incidents were rare. Life at Sawston was generally relaxed, both for the squires and for their chaplains. Ferdinand Huddleston was a moderate member of the Catholic Committee in the seventeen-eighties and in the next decade his son Richard was a member of the Cisalpine Club. Richard was on excellent terms with Anglican Fellows like the Rev. William Greenwood of St John's[4] and there is no evidence of reticence on the part of the chaplains towards such connections. With neighbouring squires too the family maintained good relations. Sawston was visited by William Cole quite as often as he visited Madingley or Horseheath. This was in the mid-eighteenth century when persecution was becoming less and less likely. Soon the Huddlestons were able to take advantage of the first tentative moves towards toleration on the part of the government. The evidence is contained in the Quarter Sessions records:

1778, 31st July. 'This day Ferdinand Huddlestone and Thomas Mitchell, Esqrs, two Roman Catholics, severally personally appeared in Court and did then and there publickly in open court take the oath appointed to be taken by an act ... for relieving his Majesty's subjects professing the Popish religion from certain penalties and disabilities.'

1791, 15th July. 'Ferdinand Huddleston of Sawston delivered into this court a certificate under his hand bearing date the fifteenth of July ... that a house or chapel situate in Sawston aforesaid is intended to be used as an assembly for religious worship by persons professing the Roman Catholic Religion and further certifying that the Revd James Taylor is the priest or minister.'[5]

The anti-Catholic disturbances of 1780 had no repercussions in Cambridgeshire, but Ferdinand's brother, Thomas, was living in London at the time and had a narrow escape during the Gordon Riots.[6]

There are a number of contemporary attempts to estimate the number of Catholics during the second half of the eighteenth century. In 1755 the Bishop of Ely's Visitation Returns found only one Catholic family in the diocese, at Sawston, as well as one individual in St Michael's parish, Cambridge.[7] There were, on the other hand, over 360 Dissenting families comprising some 1,800 individuals; even at Sawston, the sixty-six families recorded included ten Presbyterian households. In 1773 the Catholic Bishop Hornyold of the Midland District estimated the number of Catholics in Cambridgeshire at seventy.[8] Only seven English counties were credited with one hundred or fewer Catholics, Cornwall being at the bottom of the list with forty-five. Then came Cambridgeshire and Northamptonshire with seventy each, followed by Bedfordshire, Huntingdonshire, Rutland and Hertfordshire, each with between eighty and one hundred. Apart from Cornwall, therefore, the part of England with the fewest Catholics was the six contiguous counties in the east Midlands. Moreover, each of these only had one missioner; this was in marked contrast to a county like Staffordshire which had 1,760 Catholics and fourteen missioners, or even to Norfolk, with 980 Catholics and seven missioners, and Suffolk, with 360 Catholics and four missioners. In the early seventeen-eighties we do not find any reference to a greater number of Catholics, but several parishes now recorded a third or even a half of their population as Nonconformists, as at Over, for example, and at Willingham.

Little expansion could be expected in the circumstances, even given the most devoted and vigorous missioners. Priests were sometimes neither, as is shown by the case of Dom William

95

Huddleston, O.S.B., who became a convert to the Established Church in 1729. He preached his recantation sermon at Manchester[9] and in 1731 published *Irresistible Evidence against Popery*. When a Huddleston could write such a work, matters were at a low ebb indeed. From 1782 the influence of the Evangelical preacher, Charles Simeon, began to dominate the religious scene in Cambridge and at that time any chance of a Catholic revival would have seemed very remote. By 1800 there was only one priest for the four counties of Bedford, Cambridge, Buckingham and Northampton. In 1804 the Norfolk recusant, Lady Jerningham, wrote to Lady Bedingfeld; 'I have always liked Cambridge, and indeed am partial to every Regular Establishment, either Conventual or Collegial, but I do not think Cambridge a place for a Catholick priest, it is sitting too near the fire.'[10]

At that time it must have seemed obvious to any sensible observer that the Reformation had finally triumphed in this area and that the few remnants of Catholicism would soon be obliterated.

Notes and References to Chapter 5

1. *John Gerard: the Autobiography of an Elizabethan,* translated from the Latin by Philip Caraman (London, 1951), p. 33. Henry Huddleston married Dorothy, daughter of Robert, first Lord Dormer. Her cousinship with the duke of Feria was by affinity.
2. H. Foley, *Records of the English Province of the Society of Jesus* (1875–83), twelfth series, p. 536.
3. W. M. Palmer, *William Cole of Milton* (Cambridge, 1935), p. 108. For Champion's role in the life of the house, see CambRO, Huddleston MSS; JH 1/16–18; SJ 1–12, CG 1–8.
4. *Ibidem,* C3/G 19–35.
5. CambRO, Quarter Sessions Records, Q/SO8 and Q/SO9 (pp. 158 and 199), quoted from J. G. O'Leary, 'Recusants among our neighbours – Cambridge and Ely', *The Essex Recusant* 9 (1967), pp. 70–1.
6. CambRO, Huddleston MSS; C2/C16.
7. ULC, Ely Diocesan Records: B/5/3-4; B/7/1; G/1/12 folios 284-92; B/2/66.
8. W. Maziere Brady, *The Episcopal Succession in England Scotland and Ireland AD 1400 to 1875 with appointments to monasteries and extracts from consistorial acts taken from MSS in public and private libraries in Rome Florence Bologna Ravenna and Paris,* iii (Rome, 1877), p. 212.
9. William Hudleston, *A Recantation sermon preached before Samuel, Lord Bishop of Chester at the Collegiate Church in Manchester, Sept. 21. Anno Dom. 1729.* The sermon was followed by the reading of the following 'Form of Renunciation': I, William Hudleston, the eldest son living of Henry Hudleston, late of Saston [*sic*] – Hall, in the County of Cambridge, Esq;

formerly Master and Director of Studies, Secretary of the English Benedictin Order, Deputy of the General, and Deputy of the Lord Abbot of Lambspring to the General Chapter, twice appointed Representative to the Court of Rome, Deputy sent to the Pope's Nuncio in Flanders by the Provincial and Province of Canterbury and lately Confessor elect of Sion-House; do, in the presence of God and this congregation, sincerely and unfeignedly renounce the infallibility of the Church of Rome, the supremacy of the Pope, the doctrine of seven sacraments, of transubstantiation, of invocation of saints, of purgatory, of indulgence, of prayers in an unknown tongue, of merits, of justification by works, and all other errors of the said Romish Church. I do, from my heart, embrace the doctrine and principles of the Church of England, as comfortable to that of the apostolical and primitive ages. In the holy communion of this church I promise to live and die; so help me God; Wm. Hudleston.

10. *The Jerningham Letters,* edited by Egerton Castle (London, 1896), i, p. 240.

six:

The Nineteenth Century Revival of Catholicism

Attitudes to Catholicism changed in an unexpected way at the end of the eighteenth century. Just as the years following 1560 had been a time of disaster followed by remarkable successes, so were the years after the French Revolution. In political terms, Catholicism now came to be seen as the natural ally of a socially conservative Britain against the revolutionary states; no longer was a Catholic priest seen automatically as a subversive agent of absolutist Spain or rebellious Ireland. The extensive correspondence from this period conserved in the Huddleston papers shows how appalled the Catholic gentry were at the Revolution and the anti-clericalism which followed: they comment on the martyrdom of priests, the destruction of religious houses and colleges like Bornhem, the overturning of all authority in Church and State.[1] Exiled French priests were welcomed and aided by the government and, from 1793 onwards, there were often *émigré* priests at Sawston and Linton, men like Anglade, Martinet, Louvet and perhaps one John Fleury. In 1803 Fleury was with the Huddlestons at Sawston while Louvet joined a Mr Curteis at Linton.

Once again the Catholic gentry proved to be of unquestionable loyalty; Major Richard Huddleston (1768–1846) reacted to the threat of a Napoleonic invasion by enlisting in the Cambridgeshire militia and he only required special consideration for his religion by refusing to become involved in duels. The Huddlestons were thus brought into contact with the Lord Lieutenant, Hardwick, and with other leading squires like Christopher Pemberton of Trumpington; dozens of letters from the period show how firmly

98

the Huddlestons were now integrated into the county establishment, more so than at any time since the fifteen-eighties.[2] Patriotic enthusiasm even permitted the family to fight their co-religionists during the 1798 rising in Ireland.[3]

After such events, there were moves to emancipate the Catholics of both England and Ireland, an issue which was central to the politics of the first three decades of the nineteenth century.[4] The radical Cambridge editor, Benjamin Flower, had already pointed out to the Dissenters in the seventeen-nineties the inconsistency of demanding toleration for themselves while denying it to Catholics; he extended this liberal view to the Irish as well as to respectable English gentry. The Church party, however, strongly opposed such suggestions and, in the reactionary atmosphere which followed 1815, it found a voice in the Tory *Cambridge Chronicle;* this newspaper was opposed to any reform, whether in Parliament, the Corn Laws or the religious settlement. In the late eighteen-twenties, Irish affairs brought the issue once more to the forefront and the *Huntingdon, Bedford and Cambridge Weekly Journal* sought to arouse ancient prejudices; it asserted that 'the spread of the Catholic faith has uniformly been accompanied with political tyranny and mental darkness . . . a good Catholic cannot be a good servant of the public, because he owes a higher obedience to the ecclesiastical than to the civil power.' Such views were supported by the *Chronicle,* but attacked by the more radical *Independent Press.* In 1822 a Tory candidate won the borough seat by attacking emancipation and tempers reached new heights in 1826. Both town and university were bitterly divided and even after toleration was granted to Catholics in 1829, there were large and hostile demonstrations. The Rev. Moberly of Kingston was a prominent agitator and 'No Popery' slogans often appeared. These divisions continued into later decades; in the eighteen-forties the Maynooth Grant was supported by the *Independent Press,* condemned by the *Chronicle.*[5] By now emancipation had been achieved, at least in theory, and the Huddlestons could afford simply to despise 'a low-lived parson, one Mr Moberly'.

After Catholic Emancipation, families like the Huddlestons found no barrier in exercising the powers appropriate to their class; both Richard and his nephew Ferdinand (1814–90) were

Justices of the Peace and Deputy Lieutenants. But the family failed in the male line with Ferdinand's death. Sawston passed in turn to the descendants of three of his sisters; first to the Lawlers of Ireland, then to the Herberts of Clytha in Monmouthshire (an ancient recusant house), finally to its present owners, the Eyres of Leicestershire. All of them assumed the name *Huddleston.*

The gentry, with a persistence which was always admirable and sometimes heroic, had maintained Catholicism in existence in the remote countryside; by the early nineteenth century there were signs of a revival in the town and in the University of Cambridge. Since religious tests were imposed at Cambridge on proceeding to a degree only and not at matriculation, it was possible for a Catholic to come into residence if he was prepared not to take a degree (religious tests at both Oxford and Cambridge were not finally abolished until the Universities Tests Act of 1871). The first person who is recorded as having done so in the nineteenth century was George Petre of Dunkenhalgh in Lancashire, who was admitted at Jesus as a fellow commoner on 11 November 1803. He brought a chaplain who resided with him, the Rev. J. Chetwode Eustace, so that there was once again a priest in Cambridge.[6] Petre was a descendant of the Walmesleys who had owned Whittlesey manors in late Stuart times. In 1811 another Petre came, William, 11th Baron Petre, who matriculated from Christ's College at Michaelmas of that year.[7] In 1819 two brothers, Richard and Charles Acton, were admitted as fellow commoners at Magdalene; they had been brought up at Naples, where their family resided, but had both spent some time at Westminster School before coming on to Cambridge.[8] Charles stayed at Magdalene until 1823 and then went on to train for the priesthood at Rome; he later became a Cardinal, one of the four members of the Sacred College whom Cambridge can claim as its own.[9]

Soon the Catholic presence would grow considerably, but by the accession of converts. This new trend must be seen against the background of the time; things Catholic were viewed with a new sympathy in the Romantic and antiquarian atmosphere of these years, an attitude which had been prepared by the 'Gothick' fashions of the late eighteenth century, when Horace Walpole could write:

100

I doat [*sic*] on Cambridge, and could like to be often here. The beauty of King's College Chapel, now it is restored, penetrated me with a visionary longing to be a monk in it.[10]

This attitude, like the medievalism of Sir Walter Scott, was largely a literary fashion; nonetheless it was a far cry from the Protestant radicalism which had wanted to see the chapel converted into a stable. By the eighteen-twenties medieval architecture like King's College Chapel was regularly attracting high praise, despite its 'monkish' connotations and often because of them. Wordsworth's sonnet of 1820, 'Tax not the royal saint with vain expense', is the best remembered of a host of comments sympathetic to the medieval past of Cambridge. Soon this attitude was to lead to a more serious investigation of the Middle Ages and of the religion which had animated them, and this, in turn, sometimes led to an interest in the contemporary representatives of that religion.

The first conversions occurred among members of Trinity College, although the circumstances are so different in each case that it is impossible to speak of a 'movement'. The first in the series was Kenelm Henry Digby, son of a Church of Ireland Dean of Clonfert. He came up in 1815, took his B.A. in 1819 and won the Norris Prize in 1820 with an essay on the 'Evidence of the Christian Religion'. Digby was an arresting figure; he is described as 'over six feet in height, strongly built, with dark hair and eyes, a fine forehead'.[11] He was an outstanding sportsman and deserves to be remembered by posterity as one of the founders of college racing on the river;[12] he was among the first members of the Trinity Boat Club, which was formed in the Easter Term of 1825, and he rowed seven in the first eight-oared boat to be built for the Cam. This was a Trinity boat, called the *King Edward III,* which was in use by January 1826. The University Boat Club was formed in 1827 and then it was that organised racing between college boats began, to become the most characteristic and picturesque element in Cambridge sporting life.[13]

After taking his degree, Digby continued to reside in College, in rooms in Bishop's Hostel, and it is from here that he went to London at the end of 1825 to be received into the Catholic Church by Fr Scott, S.J.[14] What had prompted such a step on the part of one who came from the heart of the Anglican establishment? The fact is that Digby was a typical Romantic. When he was an undergraduate, he had resolved to be a knight and, getting into King's College Chapel at nightfall, had kept vigil there until dawn. During the Long Vacations, he travelled abroad through the main Catholic countries of Europe, Belgium, France, Italy, Germany, Austria, Switzerland; on these journeys he indulged two passions, love of the Middle Ages and of swimming. He plunged into the Danube, the Elbe and the Rhine, and he even swam in the Tiber, much to the surprise of the natives. He was impressed by the devotion of congregations at mass and he began to see, present in the liturgy of the Catholic Church, the supernatural principle which had enchanted him in what he knew of the Middle Ages. When he was back in College he read extensively in Wren's magnificent library, St Augustine and Bossuet and the history of the English Reformation. Then he began to write; in 1822 he published two parts of a book which he called *The Broadstone of Honour* and he describes how eagerly he used to wait in Trumpington Street for the arrival of the mail coach which brought the proof sheets from the printers in London.[15] It is a discursive, rambling compilation, full of stories of knights and crusaders and the legends of saints, interspersed with descriptions of scenery and architecture, but it appealed to the aspirations of the age. Like Chateaubriand, Digby made Catholicism attractive because he showed that it is beautiful.

In the Michaelmas Term of 1826 Digby was joined at Trinity by another convert, Ambrose Phillipps (who later assumed the name Phillipps de Lisle).[16] Phillipps had become a Catholic the previous year at the age of sixteen, partly under the influence of an *émigré* priest who taught French at his school. De Lisle had rooms in Nevile's Court and he and Digby, who seem to have been the only Catholics in the university, soon became friends. They used to ride to Ware in Hertfordshire on Sundays to attend mass at Old Hall, where St Edmund's College had made its home after having been driven out of Douai by the Revolution. Presumably they preferred the liturgy as it was celebrated in a seminary to the domestic scale of the worship at Sawston, but it was quite a sacrifice. Old Hall is twenty-five miles from Cambridge and they had to fast from midnight if they wanted to receive Holy Communion at mass. To one who has swum across the Rhine, such endurance presented no problem but de Lisle was of a more delicate constitution. After eighteen months his lungs were affected and a severe haemoptysis cut short his Cambridge career; he left in the spring of 1828 and had to spend the next two winters in Italy to recover. However, his influence among his contemporaries had been considerable; his enthusiasm had ensured that Catholic doctrines were once more discussed in Cambridge. The new Catholics were also in touch with the Huddlestons; over one hundred letters to Richard Huddleston survive, written between 1826 and 1845 by Digby, who was a frequent visitor at Sawston.[17]

The third Trinity man to become a Catholic was George Spencer, but in his case conversion came after he had left Cambridge.[18] He was the youngest son of the second Earl Spencer and came up in 1817; he seems to have known Digby slightly[19] but he belonged to the 'smart set' in College and showed no interest in the Middle Ages so that there was no affinity between them at the time. Spencer was ordained in the Church of England and became Rector of Brington, near Althorp. He had left Trinity before de Lisle arrived but they met in 1829 and it was largely through his influence that Spencer was received into the Catholic Church in 1830. He soon decided to go to the English College in Rome and, on the way, met Digby in Paris; they became lifelong friends. Spencer worked as a secular priest at Walsall, West Bromwich and Oscott before joining the Passionist Order. He died, after an active life as a missioner, in 1864. De Lisle is best remembered as the founder of a Cistercian Abbey, Mount St Bernard, which he established in 1835 near his estate of Grace-Dieu in Leicestershire; he died in 1878 and Digby in 1880.

Meanwhile Bishop Milner of the Midland District had been trying to establish a Catholic church in Cambridge; he was unsuccessful in this up to the time of his death in 1826. Efforts continued with an appeal in the *Laity's Directory* for 1828 by the Rev. Edward Huddleston, chaplain at Sawston, who mentioned 'the celebrity of the place, the daily increasing number of resident Irish Catholics and the fact of there being no public chapel in the whole county.' He asks for funds for 'this arduous and destitute Mission'.[20] Such appeals were to be repeated frequently in the next few years, both by Huddleston and his successor, John Scott, who mentioned as an additional inducement to generosity the moral and religious danger to the undergraduate sons of the Catholic gentry. One such was Thomas Redington from Galway who was admitted fellow commoner at Christ's College on 16 March 1832 at the age of sixteen, having come up from Oscott. He matriculated in the Michaelmas Term 1832 and kept ten terms at Cambridge, although he could not proceed to a degree at the end of them; his presence, however, considerably diminished the moral and religious danger of the other Catholic undergraduates since his mother came to live in Cambridge and brought her chaplain, an Irish priest. She rented a house where mass was said on Sundays for the Catholics of Cambridge.[21] In 1836 the appeals were still being made, apparently without success, though the scheme had the support of Bishop Walsh, the successor of Milner as Vicar Apostolic of the Midland District. These attempts took place in the context of a general increase of population in the town; between 1801 and 1901 it rose from 10,000 to 40,000 and the increase occurred almost entirely outside the traditional parish structure of the centre, in the straggling parish of St Andrew the Less, covering Barnwell and the Newmarket Road, and in the slums to the south, around Union Road.

The need for a Catholic church was becoming pressing and it looked for a time as if the Jesuits would found one; why they did not do so is unclear, although Bishop Walsh writes in general terms of 'a little temporary opposition'.[22] Eventually in 1841 the Rev. B. Shanley, a secular priest from the Irish College in Paris, was sent to Cambridge and this was the first step in the establishment of a permanent mission in the town. Fr Shanley began by ministering to a group of Irish harvesters settled in the Barnwell area, where he said mass in a cottage. Richard Huddleston strongly supported him financially and bought land in Union Road for the building of a church. There was great indignation in the university when this project became known and on 5 November 1841 a large group of students gathered in Union Road to tear up the foundations. Fortunately the mayor appeared with a force

104

of special constables and a body of burly Irishmen also arrived so that the students dispersed without doing any damage.[23]

Eventually a Catholic church was opened in Cambridge in 1842. It was dedicated to St Andrew and was designed by A. W. Pugin. This church survives at St Ives, whither it was removed brick by brick after the present church was opened in 1890; a wooden figure of St Andrew on his cross also survives from the first church and is in the north transept of the present church. Bishop Wareing, Vicar Apostolic of the newly created Eastern District, consecrated the church on St George's Day 1843, the sermon being preached by Bishop Wiseman. The first rector of St Andrew's was Canon Thomas Quinlivan; throughout the difficult early years he and his congregation were under the patronage and the protection of the Huddlestons,[24] so that the church in Cambridge can be seen as the direct successor of the old Catholicism of Sawston which had survived the long and secret centuries to emerge thus unexpectedly into the light of common day. Within Cambridge things were changing for the Church. Firstly, the number of Catholics was rising as the town's trade and industry grew; the religious census of 1851 indicated that Cambridge had a population of 28,000, which included 260 Catholics who had attended mass on census Sunday. Secondly, the composition of Catholicism in England was changing as it acquired a wider social basis than country squires on the one hand and Irish labourers on the other.

Digby and de Lisle had led the way in introducing a new element into English Catholicism. A little less than ten years after their conversion the Oxford Movement began, and it shared many of the motives which had led to the conversion of the Cambridge men a decade earlier. These were an interest in the Church of the Middle Ages, a quest for Christian continuity and a search for authority in religion other than the parliamentary statutes which governed the Church of England. How legitimate was it to introduce into the Church of England customs from the medieval liturgy, and, if that were allowed, was it permissible to introduce contemporary Catholic devotions? In the eighteen-thirties such innovations seemed possible. There was antiquarianism mixed with piety; High Anglicans sympathised with groups like the

Cambridge Camden Society, instituted in 1839, which aimed to restore churches to what was imagined to have been their medieval appearance. Cambridge produced a *cause célèbre* when the Round Church was restored. A stone altar was put in to complete the impression of authenticity and yet this was opposed as 'popish' by the incumbent; when the Court of Arches upheld the incumbent by a judgment of 21 January 1845, the Society received a blow from which it never recovered.

Two questions arose in an acute form. Was the Church of England enough of a *via media* to incorporate these changes in a Catholic direction? and, Did these changes imply a view of the Church and of Christianity which could only be satisfied by incorporation into the wider ecclesiastical reality of which Rome was the centre? In the eighteen-forties an additional question arose concerning the right of the State, in virtue of the Royal Supremacy, to determine doctrine by Act of Parliament and to regulate liturgical practice through the Courts of Law. As conservative Protestants had long feared, there now began a marked movement of conversions to Roman Catholicism, of which that of John Henry Newman on 9 October 1845 was only the most celebrated. The role of Cambridge in this movement deserves to be better appreciated. It is called the Oxford Movement because the Oxford Tractarians were its leaders but the ensuing Movement affected both the ancient universities. In 1842 de Lisle had been 'very sanguine' about conversions from the ranks of the Puseyites, though Digby was 'sick of them' and wanted 'to know no more of them till they became Catholics'. In 1845 Digby conveys the atmosphere of the time when he writes, 'Two Cambridge University men were on the "Comet" with me that day from Sawston. Their talk was of copes and chasubles, Divine Offices, etc. They denounced the State calumnies of the Jesuits, etc. I said nothing. . . .'[25]

De Lisle was right to be sanguine. In 1884 W. Gordon-Gorman published *Rome's Recruits or Converts to Rome: a list of over 3000 Protestants who have become Roman Catholics since the commencement of the 19th century.* The list includes three hundred men from the University of Oxford, a large number as is to be expected, but Cambridge provides 149, a remarkable figure for a university dominated by scepticism and evangelicalism. Moreover, sixty of these were Trinity men, a larger number than that provided by any other college at either Oxford or Cambridge. At Cambridge, St John's College follows with fourteen converts. The dates of conversion are not always given but in most cases it is clear that conversion occurred after departure from the university. A picture emerges from this list of a large-scale drift in the eighteen-forties; thus twenty-three names of Cambridge graduates are recorded for the period 1844–50 and twelve for the period 1851–60. After that there is a trickle, five names for 1861–70 and seven for 1871–80. The trickle was aided by the continuance of the Anglo-Catholic movement in the Church of England.

The first conversions of this second group of Cambridge converts caused a considerable stir and they were not uninfluenced by the first group, Digby and de Lisle. John Morris came up to Trinity in October, 1845; he had had as private tutor before coming to Cambridge a former Fellow of Trinity, Henry Alford, Vicar of Wymeswold in Leicestershire. Alford, who was later to become Dean of Canterbury, was much influenced by the Tractarians and he brought his pupil to visit de Lisle who took them over Mount St Bernard Abbey. Morris began a lengthy correspondence with de Lisle on religious matters and, once he got to Cambridge, he came under the influence of Frederick Apthorp Paley who supervised him in Classics. Paley was a Johnian, not a Fellow but an M.A., resident in college; he was one of the first members of the Cambridge Camden Society and he introduced Morris to Fr Quinlivan, who is described in reminiscences of that period written by T. Field as 'the clever, popular, excellent and very wide-awake Romish priest then resident in the town.'[26] By November Morris was writing to Alford that he intended to become a Catholic; this provoked Alford into writing a text, published early in 1846 with the alluring title *An Earnest Dissuasive from Joining the Communion of the Church of Rome addressed to the younger members of the Church of England and especially to Students in the Universities*. It was a worthy composition which refrained from entering into controversy or imputing unworthy motives to those who had gone over to Rome but it developed the argument, unlikely to appeal to the young, that they were too immature to judge the Church into which they had been baptized. It was no use; by the Easter Term Paley and Morris were having tea with Bishop Wareing, who was on a visit to Cambridge, and on 20 May 1846 Wareing received Morris into the Catholic Church at Northampton. By 18 June the fact was reported in *The Times,* which added with relish that 'stringent measures are, it is said, about to be adopted in order to stop any further movement in the same direction.' An interest in ecclesiastical architecture was one thing but conversions to Rome were altogether different. As far as the Establishment were concerned, there were limits and the conversion of a Cambridge undergraduate was one of them. Field wrote of 'the scandal . . . of an undergraduate lapsing in mid-term to Rome'.[27] It would not have been so bad in the Vacation.

The fur really began to fly that October as the correspondence columns of *The Times* gradually dragged into the controversy Alford, Pugin, de Lisle and Wareing. Eventually the general ire fell on the unfortunate Paley, who, having also become a Catholic, was turned out of his college; he then worked as tutor in various families, including that of Kenelm Digby, but came back to Cambridge from 1860 to 1874 as private tutor, leaving for the second time to become Professor of Classical Literature in Cardinal Manning's short-lived Catholic University College, Kensington. Morris did not return to the university but went to the English College in Rome where he was ordained in 1849. He later entered the Society of Jesus.[28]

In October 1847 another future convert arrived in Cambridge, Thomas Edward Bridgett, who matriculated at St John's; he stayed for three years and did not become a Catholic until just after leaving, being received at the London Oratory on 12 June 1850. His journey towards the Catholic Church was different from that of Morris; he records in his reminiscences, written thirty years later, that he never met any Catholics before being received but that his 'day of grace' came when he picked up one of the books of Kenelm Digby in a bookseller's. He also records the influence on him of a visit to the little Catholic church in Cambridge which had been opened four years before his arrival in the university:

Among the causes which led me towards the Church were some very simple words spoken by a poor Irish labourer. I was then studying at the University of Cambridge, and a fellow-student had invited me to visit the Catholic Chapel. It was a very small building in an obscure street in the suburbs of the town, and we had some difficulty in finding it. We got the keys from a poor Catholic man, who lived near, and after we had looked at the Church, my friend, who was fond of a joke, began to banter the poor Irishman. 'Why, Paddy' he said, 'do you think you've got the truth all to yourselves down in this little back street, and all our learned doctors and divines in this University are in error?' The answer that Paddy gave was this 'Well, sir, I suppose they're very learned, but they can't agree together, while we are all one.'[29]

Because of the tests, Bridgett did not proceed to a degree. He joined the Redemptorist Order and was ordained in 1856.

In the eighteen-seventies particularly 'high' churches in Cambridge included St Clement's (the vicar of this church had been converted in 1857), Little St Mary's and the new church of St Giles built in 1875. The painted glass in St Giles is a fascinating expression of the Anglo-Catholic view of history; its windows propose to the devotion of the faithful a series starting in the south aisle with St Clement, St Ignatius of Antioch and St Cyprian and going on, through the Venerable Bede and King Alfred, to St Katherine of Siena, King Henry VI, St Teresa of Avila, King Charles I Martyr, Bishop Samuel Seabury and Bishop Charles Gore.

There was even a new Catholic presence in the countryside since the Hon. Frederica North of Kirtling Towers, near Newmarket, had built a Catholic church at Kirtling. It was made of corrugated iron but was replaced in 1876 by the present stone building, dedicated to Our Lady Immaculate and St Philip Neri. The husband of the foundress was the descendant of a squire whose fortune had been established on monastic spoils; in 1879 he too became a Catholic and in 1884 succeeded to the peerage as 11th Baron North de Kirtling. The Anglican incumbent then had to face the problem of what to do when the squire was of a different religion. Some friction did occur; by the turn of the century there were some ten Catholics in the parish yet the vicar continued to regard it as an area of Protestant loyalties where, for example, all households should receive Anglican literature. The ensuing argument was a small affair but it illustrates the existence of a problem which could not have occurred in the previous three centuries.[30]

The presence of these new Catholics encouraged the optimistic view that the conversion of England was not too distant. This was the atmosphere at the time of the 'Papal Aggression' of 1850, i.e. the creation by Pius IX of a territorial hierarchy in England and Wales; Cambridge found itself in the new diocese of Northampton, a large and impoverished diocese under Bishop William Wareing. Naturally there was a storm of outraged Protestant feelings; one of Edward Huddleston's friends wrote: 'What a tremendous hurricane is now growing against poor Papists.'[31]

Notes and References to Chapter 6

1. Camb RO, Huddleston MSS; C3/M16-26; B 14, 58.
2. *Ibidem*, C3/HR 1–53; C2/P12.
3. *Ibidem*, C2/HD 205.
4. *Ibidem*, C1/EH 88.
5. See M. J. Murphy, *Cambridge Newspapers and Opinion 1780-1850* (Cambridge, Oleander Press, 1977), pp. 71–3.
6. Venn, *Al.Can.*, part II, v, p. 102. B. Ward, *The Eve of Catholic Emancipation* (London, 1911), i, p. 213.
7. Venn, *Al.Can.*, part II, v, p. 102.
8. *DNB*. Venn, *Al.Can.*, part II, i, p. 6.
9. The others are Cardinal Beaufort (Peterhouse 1388–9); Cardinal Fisher (mentioned above, pp. 58–69); and Cardinal Howard (mentioned above, p. 85). The friar, William Peyto, who had been a Fellow of Queens' before becoming a Franciscan, was created a Cardinal by Paul IV in 1557 but declined the hat.
10. *The Letters of Horace Walpole Fourth Earl of Orford,* edited by P. Cunningham (London, 1891), vi, p. 441. Letter of 22 May, 1777.
11. B. Holland, *Memoir of Kenelm Henry Digby* (London, 1919), p. 10.
12. Digby had begun rowing on the Thames when he was at school at Petersham. When he came up to Cambridge he found only inferior 'tubs' on the Cam so he and a group of friends had a four-oared boat built and went out regularly from 1816 onwards; *ibidem*, pp. 7–9, and W. W. Rouse Ball, *Cambridge Notes,* 2nd edition (Cambridge, 1921), p. 312.
13. St John's College followed closely on Trinity in the foundation of its boat club, the Lady Margaret, which was in existence by the Michaelmas Term of 1825. It was the L.M.B.C. which first rowed an eight on the Cam but this

was a boat built for the schoolboys of Eton and imported by St John's. The T.B.C. commissioned the first eight built for use on the Cam and designed for undergraduates; it was built by King's of Oxford. Cf W.W. Rouse Ball, *The Early History of First Trinity* [n.p.], 1922, pp. 4–6; *History of the First Trinity Boat Club* (Cambridge, 1908), pp. 1–14.

14. B. Holland, *Memoir of Kenelm Henry Digby,* pp. 34–43.
15. *Ibidem,* p. 61.
16. For de Lisle's Cambridge career, see E. S. Purcell, *Life and Letters of Ambrose Phillipps de Lisle* (London, 1900), i, pp. 32–6.
17. CambRO, Huddleston MSS; C3/DG 1–106, especially 17.
18. U. Young, *Life of Father Ignatius Spencer C.P.* (London, 1933), pp. 10–42.
19. B. Holland, *Memoir of Kenelm Henry Digby,* p. 47.
20. P. S. Wilkins, *The Church of Our Lady and the English Martyrs Cambridge* (Cambridge, 1965), p. 5.
21. *Ibidem,* pp. 7–8; Venn, *Al.Can.,* part II, v, p. 264.
22. P. S. Wilkins, *Our Lady and the English Martyrs,* p. 8.
23. *Ibidem,* p. 9.
24. See CambRO, Huddleston MSS; C1/EH 61–73 for some of Quinlivan's letters from this period.
25. *Ibidem,* C3/DG 83, 104.
26. Thomas Field, 'Reminiscences of F. A. Paley', *The Eagle: A Magazine supported by Members of St John's College* 15 (1889), p. 446.
27. *Ibidem.*
28. For details of Morris's life and conversion see Venn, *Al.Can.,* part II, iv, p. 471; J. H. Pollen, *The Life and Letters of Father John Morris of the Society of Jesus 1826–1893* (London, 1896); *Life journals and letters of Henry Alford D.D. late Dean of Canterbury,* ed. by his widow. 3rd. ed. (London, 1874), pp. 151–3.
29. C. Ryder, *Life of Thomas Edward Bridgett Priest of the Congregation of the Most Holy Redeemer with Characteristics from his writings* (London, 1906), p. 12. See also Venn, *Al.Can.,* part II, i, p. 378.
30. CambRO, Huddleston MSS; P101/3/9–10, 1905.
31. *Ibidem,* EH 16.

seven:

Consolidation in Town and University

Once again the unexpected happened.[1] The establishment of the Hierarchy in 1850 caused an uproar but, once the sound and fury had died down, nothing more damaging had occurred than a series of snide cartoons in *Punch* and Lord John Russell's Ecclesiastical Titles Act, which was a dead letter from the start. Once the hurricane had blown over, Catholics had the solid advantage of a diocesan structure all over the country, each diocese being a focus for the consolidation and development of the parishes. In Cambridge, Canon Quinlivan retired in 1883 from the church of St Andrew and was replaced by Canon Christopher Scott, who arrived with instructions from Bishop Riddell of Northampton to build a more fitting church.

The Parishes

Canon Scott was a native of Cambridge who had been received into the Catholic Church as a young man. After studies at the English College in Rome, he had had wide pastoral experience, including eighteen years as the Administrator of the cathedral at Northampton. He was a man of vision and taste, fond of music

18 (opposite). Our Lady and the English Martyrs: view from Downing College. The church was designed by Dunn and Hansom of Newcastle and built 1885–90. The spire is 214 ft high, about the same height as the west tower of Ely, and is a Cambridge landmark. (Photograph by Andrew Gough)

113

and well versed in the classics. He could see that Catholics would soon be coming to the university in considerable numbers and he wanted to build a church not unworthy of the academic past of Cambridge. He found the means to do so through a pious French lady with an unusual past. Pauline Duvernay had been a famous ballerina in Paris and London in the earlier part of the century but in 1845 she had married Stephen Lyne-Stephens, a wealthy landowner, and had become lady of the manor at Lynford Hall, near Brandon. In 1861 Mrs Lyne-Stephens became a widow and devoted most of her wealth thereafter to charitable causes. Canon Scott had met her when he was Vicar Capitular of the diocese in 1879–80 and she had told him then of her desire to build a Catholic church. A site had been acquired at Cambridge through the donation of £3,000 by the Duke of Norfolk, which had paid for half the cost, and in 1884 Mrs Lyne-Stephens promised to build the church and presbytery at Cambridge, a project which eventually cost £70,000.

The new parish church at Cambridge was begun in 1885 and completed in 1890. The architects were Dunn and Hansom of Newcastle and the builders Rattee and Kett of Cambridge. It is a magnificent church in the Decorated style of gothic beloved by the Victorians, built to impress rather than to accommodate a large congregation, which was lacking at the time. Over the crossing is a lofty lantern tower, 118 feet high; its eight traceried windows shed an abundance of light on the sanctuary. The belfry tower in the west end of the church is even more impressive, as the stone spire rises to 214 feet. It is one of the landmarks of Cambridge. Canon Scott believed in didactic sculpture so that statues and inscriptions illustrative of Catholic doctrine and devotion abound; sometimes unwary visitors accepted from Canon

19 (opposite). Our Lady and the English Martyrs: crossing and apse. The lantern tower over the crossing is 118 ft high. The spiral staircase of the south east corner is surmounted by a statue of Our Lady with a group of statues of attendant angels immediately below it. There are many carved inscriptions on the exterior of the church; the words of the Ave Maria *can be seen on the parapet above the apse.* (Photograph by Alan Rooke)

Scott the offer of being shown round the church and found themselves embarked on a lecture tour of two hours. The coronation of Our Lady is on the gable of the west front and, on the transom of the north porch, a fine statue of St John Fisher in cardinal's robes (see plate 21). The words of the Hail Mary in Latin are carved in large letters round the apse and the north side of the nave, while the north transept, overlooking the busy traffic of Hills Road, proclaims: *Pray for the good estate of Yolande Marie Louise Lyne-Stephens Foundress of this church.*

The interior is equally lavish. It is entirely vaulted in stone and there is a wealth of carving on the capitals and roof bosses. The composition is dominated by the great rood, with the figures of Our Lady and St John on either side, and by the delicate carved baldachino over the high altar. There is a definite university slant to the iconography; two windows in the gallery above the porch represent symbolically the dedications of the colleges; the south aisle windows, destroyed by a bomb in 1941 but replaced according to the original scheme, portray the story of St John Fisher, starting (in the window nearest to the west door) with Henry VII and Lady Margaret Beaufort attending mass in King's College Chapel. It is possible that the inclusion in the plan of a lofty ante-chapel was intended in imitation of some college chapels. Certainly the building of a large presbytery next to the church, in a Tudoresque red brick style characteristic of much academic building of the period, indicates that Canon Scott expected it to be thronged in due course by Catholic undergraduates and dons. It must have been a proud day for him when the new church was consecrated on 8 October 1890. A week later Bishop Riddell sang the first high mass there in the presence of most of the Catholic bishops of England. The whole style of the church proclaimed that

20 (opposite). Our Lady and the English Martyrs: interior. The Rood shows Our Lord as King with Our Lady and St John on either side; it was carved locally by B. McLean Leach in 1914. Above the sanctuary arch is a painting of Christ in Glory by Westlake. The baldachino over the old high altar is carved in wood. Under the crossing is the new altar table put in place in 1973. (Photograph by Alan Rooke)

Catholics intended to come back to Cambridge not with a whimper but a bang; the new dedication, Our Lady and the English Martyrs, showed that they were not sparing of Protestant susceptibilities. On the university side there must have been pained surprise at the splendour and self-assertiveness of the new Catholic church. The witticism of a don at King's went the round of the combination rooms; Mr Lyne-Stephens was reputed to have made a part of his considerable fortune from the manufacture of dolls' eyes, 'so now the money derived from dolls' eyes is to be devoted to the cult of idols.'

The later development of the parish followed what could be called growth by cell-division; mass centres were established in outlying parts of the parish and, when the congregations had increased sufficiently to support a priest, new parishes were set up. Thus a tin hut was built in old Chesterton in 1938, a priest went to live there in 1945 and in 1958 the present church of St Laurence was built in Milton Road. Sawston was served for a long time from Cambridge until a priest went to live in a house given by the owner of the hall in 1958 and a church was built in the same year. St Philip Howard's, Cherry Hinton, acquired a permanent building and a resident priest in 1978.

With the churches came the schools. Canon Quinlivan started a school in a cottage in Union Road in 1843. It was called officially the Union Road Roman Catholic School, though everybody called it St Andrew's once the church was built. New buildings were put up in 1868 and extended in 1894. In 1936 the school was rebuilt and then re-named St Andrew's only to have the name changed to St Alban's in 1962 to avoid confusion with another school. Baron Anatole von Hügel, who will be mentioned frequently in the story of the Catholic revival in the university,

21. Statue of St John Fisher on the transom of the (architectural) north porch of Our Lady and the English Martyrs Church, Hills Road. Statue by Boulton of Cheltenham, showing Fisher the Bishop, wearing the rochet, mozetta and cross. The heads on either side of the porch (not shown) portray Cardinal Manning and Bishop Riddell. (Photographs by Andrew Gough)

took a regular interest in this school; he and his wife are referred to frequently in the school's logbooks. They gave a party to the children twice a year, at Christmas and Midsummer; every first communicant was presented with a prayer book while Baroness von Hügel came into the classroom to keep an eye on the girls' sewing. Much later came the Catholic Secondary School, St Bede's at Cherry Hinton, opened in 1962. Another primary school, St Laurence's, was started on the Arbury estate in 1968.

The religious orders came too; in 1898 the Sisters of the Institute of the Blessed Virgin Mary opened St Mary's School in Bateman Street as a boarding and day school for girls. The Carmelites founded a house of contemplative nuns at Chesterton in 1923; this moved to Waterbeach in 1937 and faded out in 1973 when the remaining nuns were merged with the Carmelite community at Chichester. The Sisters of the Holy Family of Bordeaux started the Hope Nursing Home in Brooklands Avenue in 1944, having begun their nursing work in Cambridge four years earlier in a rented house in Bateman Street.

The University Chaplaincy

Canon Scott was right in his forecast that Catholics would soon come back to the university but he was mistaken in thinking that they would come to the parish church. It was in 1856 that the Cambridge University Act had allowed non-Anglicans to become members of colleges and to proceed to their first degree, though they were still excluded from fellowships, a disability which was removed in 1871. Hardly, however, had the obstacles to the attendance of Catholics been removed by the university than they were re-introduced by the Church. In 1867, at the instigation of Cardinal Manning, the Congregation of Propaganda in Rome issued a directive to the English bishops that parents should be dissuaded from sending their sons to the ancient universities, *Universitates Anglicanae* as it called them, because of the danger to their faith.[2] There was a good deal of dismay among the laity at the time[3] and, after Manning's death in 1892, opposition to the policy of exclusion was so general that Cardinal Vaughan realised that the Hierarchy would have to change its policy; largely at the

120

instigation of Baron Anatole von Hügel, he persuaded the bishops to petition Rome to remove the prohibition. This was done by a decree of Propaganda of 1 April 1895; it stated that, owing to changed circumstances, Catholic youths might go to Oxford and Cambridge, as there was not yet a Catholic university, although this was still seen as the goal to be reached *quam primum fieri possit*. However certain safeguards were to accompany this relaxation; among these should be regular courses of lectures given by Catholic professors on philosophy, history and religion. A special committee was to be formed, composed of bishops, priests and laymen, to raise funds for these lectures and to appoint the professors.

As a result of these directives the bishops set up the Universities' Catholic Education Board[4] to implement the mandate from Rome. It was clear to everyone in England that it was impossible to finance what would have been virtually the creation of a Catholic faculty at Oxford and Cambridge, nor was it considered likely that Catholics would attend such lectures. Instead it was decided to appoint a chaplain at both universities to look after Catholic undergraduates and to take what steps they should consider practical to put into effect the Roman mandate. So it was that on 16 January 1896 the Rev. Edmund Nolan, Vice-President of St Edmund's College, Ware, was appointed the first Catholic chaplain at Cambridge.

In spite of the bishops' prohibition, there were already a number of Catholics at the university. Baron Anatole von Hügel, brother of the more famous Friedrich, had been Curator of the Museum of Archaeology since 1883 and had been largely instrumental in securing from the bishops a change of attitude towards admission to the universities. In 1887 he had presided at the setting up of a Church Maintenance Association, a grouping of Catholic members of the university for the support of the church (it had perforce to be the parish church then) and for mutual encouragement; in 1899 it became the Cambridge University Catholic Association (henceforth referred to as C.U.C.A.), with the more specific aim of providing accommodation for the university oratory and chaplain. Evennett, in his study of the events leading up to 1895, has calculated that there were probably not more than a dozen

Catholic undergraduates resident in any one year before 1895;[5] even afterwards the numbers did not go up appreciably.

Meanwhile, Fr Nolan's arrival in Cambridge had been attended by complications. Bishop Riddell of Northampton had been opposed to any change of policy but, once the change had been made, he considered that it was for the local bishop to make the appointment. He wrote to inform Nolan on 19 April 1896 that he had appointed Canon Scott to be the chaplain; that splendid church in Hills Road was not to be wasted. While Cardinal Vaughan appealed to Rome for a verdict, Nolan went to live at the Presbytery, which says much for the equanimity of the 'Chaplain' and the 'Anti-Chaplain', as Garrett Sweeney wittily calls them in his history of St Edmund's House.[6] Rome's reply came on 10 June 1896; chaplains to Catholics in universities were to be appointed by the English bishops as a whole, but their faculties were to be granted by the local Ordinary. Bishop Riddell had lost.

The other complication was that Fr Nolan soon found himself not only chaplain but also Master of St Edmund's House. While at Ware he had approached von Hügel to find out how students from the college could be matriculated for a degree at Cambridge. Von Hügel, always a visionary and a schemer, formed the project for a house of studies for priests and candidates for the priesthood at Cambridge. In his mind it could provide a base for the chaplain and also those lecturers required by Rome as a safeguard for the faith. In an amazingly short time premises were found, since the Duke of Norfolk once again provided funds to purchase a building, surely the ugliest in Cambridge, originally put up as a Private Hostel by the Rev. William Ayerst in 1895. Here Fr Nolan set up house in November 1896 with half a dozen students; the chapel was designated by the Hierarchy as the chapel for Catholic undergraduates at the university.

It was in this chapel that the first of the lectures prescribed by Rome was given on 15 November 1896 by Dom Cuthbert Butler, who had just taken up residence at Benet House, the Downside house of studies at Cambridge; this was yet another institution brought into being with the warm encouragement of Anatole von Hügel, who had seen it for a time as the place to provide the lecturers for Catholic undergraduates.[7] Gradually the solution adopted by the chaplains in the discharge of their obligation of providing instruction for Catholics at the university came to be the following: a talk of half-an-hour, on a higher level than a parish sermon could be, given by a visiting personality and not by the chaplain, and supplementary to the two Sunday morning masses. Undergraduates were told that attendance at these was a condition of their being at Cambridge with episcopal approval; these talks came to be called, somewhat oddly, conferences, presumably from the Italian *conferenza,* a lecture.

By October 1899, the number of Catholic members of the university having increased to forty-five, it was felt that St Edmund's was too remote from the centre of Cambridge and two rooms on Green Street were rented by C.U.C.A. to serve as a chapel and a meeting place for students. They had formed a literary and debating society for Catholics in 1895, with fifteen founder members, and had called it the Fisher Society. In 1902 Fr Nolan left Cambridge to become the President of Prior Park, Bath, and from that time the chaplaincy and St Edmund's House parted company; Fr Arthur Stapylton Barnes became chaplain.

Fr Barnes had been at University College, Oxford, and became a clergyman on retiring from the army; in 1895 he was received into the Catholic Church and was later ordained in Rome by Cardinal Merry del Val. On his arrival at Cambridge, he saw at once that a chaplain must have a house of his own and took the lease of Llandaff House in Regent Street, a building now demolished. Robert Hugh Benson spent a year at Llandaff House in 1904-5 and this is a description of the chaplaincy of these days written by his brother, A. C. Benson:

> Llandaff House is a big, rather mysterious mansion in the main street of Cambridge, opposite the University Arms Hotel . . . the front rooms of the big, two gabled house are mostly shop; but the back of the house remains a stately little residence, with a chapel, a garden with some fine trees, and opens on to the extensive and quiet park of Downing College.[8]

Fr Barnes was soon made a Monsignor, and this foreign sounding title, usually abbreviated to *Mgr,* was so unfamiliar to Cambridge that it gave rise to the nickname of *Mugger*. In spite of a certain rotundity of speech, Mugger Barnes was on the undergraduate wavelength; it was he who said, 'All undergraduates lose their faith at eighteen and regain it at twenty-one.'[9] He also hit upon what was to prove the essential of university chaplaincy development in England; that is, the presence of a priest, not engaged on teaching or on parish work and not belonging to an institution, readily available to see students at any hour of the day or night in his own house. Writing sixty years later, Fr Michael Hollings expressed the essential of the chaplaincy ideal in terms which could equally well have applied to Mugger Barnes's chaplaincy: 'The effort within the chaplaincy as I know it is to have an open house, with anyone able to walk in to see the chaplain, without ringing a bell, and without disclosing his or her arrival. This is from 7 a.m. till midnight or after.'[10]

In this setting the Fisher Society continued to flourish and in 1911 it organised a great dinner in honour of Cardinal Bourne, who had just been made a member of the Sacred College. Characteristically, Mugger Barnes considered this event as the peak of his tenure of the chaplaincy; dinners have always had their importance in Cambridge.

In 1916 Mgr Barnes left the Cambridge chaplaincy on a mission to the United States and on his return he was appointed chaplain at Oxford, where he remained until 1926. As there were few undergraduates at Cambridge because of the war, he was not immediately replaced there. In 1918 Fr James Bernard Marshall, M.C., became the chaplain; he had been at Brasenose College, Oxford, and was a barrister before becoming a priest. The lease of Llandaff House having run out, he began to group Catholics, first at 50 Bridge Street, where he rented rooms, and then at 2 Round Church Street, a house of which the Cambridge Union was the landlord. The small numbers made it possible to celebrate mass in two bedrooms on the first floor which had been joined together to form a chapel; the choir would take up their position on Sundays in an adjoining room and sing the mass at the congregation through a hole in the wall.

Fr Marshall left the chaplaincy in the middle of an academic year because of a series of circumstances set in motion by a taxi in Trafalgar Square. The taxi knocked down Canon Scott who died on 17 February 1922 and the Bishop appointed Fr Marshall as parish priest to Our Lady and the English Martyrs. The Oxford and Cambridge Catholic Education Board then had to recommend a replacement at short notice and it was Fr C. C. Martindale, S.J., who suggested Fr John Lopes, then preaching a mission at Birmingham as a member of the Catholic Missionary Society.

Outram Evennett, who later became Fellow of Trinity and President of C.U.C.A., was an undergraduate at the time of Fr Lopes's arrival at Cambridge, which he describes thus:

> Carrying a stout bag in each hand, he appeared at the Parish Hall where a concert was in progress, dropped his bags on the floor and said: 'I'm exhausted, my dears, where do I have to go from here?' It was a remarkable entry and clearly someone remarkable had arrived. From his earliest days an air of extravaganza hung about the Chaplaincy.[11]

It was not just the arrival of a new chaplain but the start of a new era for the chaplaincy.

John Ludlow Lopes was a remarkable personality. He came from a family of Portuguese Jewish origins which had migrated to England in the early nineteenth century via Jamaica. It had become Anglican and eventually progressed so far in the Establishment as to acquire a baronetcy and two peerages.[12] John came from a younger branch which had however inherited a considerable proportion of the family's wealth. He was educated privately and then went to Exeter College, Oxford. On leaving Oxford in 1905 he decided to train for the ministry of the Church of England and went for a year to Ely Theological College under Berkeley William Randolph (Principal, 1891-1911). He always remained devoted to the memory of Randolph and Ely.

John Lopes began his ministry as curate of St Basil's, Birmingham, a basilica-like edifice now no longer used as a church, and he went to live in a tenement in a down-town quarter of Deritend. But, and this is characteristically Lopesian, he spent a considerable amount on putting oak panelling and bottle-green leaded windows into his down-town tenement. What the parishioners made of it is not recorded and, in any case, the stay at

Deritend was short; in 1917 John Lopes was received into the Catholic Church. After studies in Rome, he was ordained and worked at the English Martyrs, Sparkhill, Birmingham, until he joined the Catholic Missionary Society.

Fr Lopes, even when young, was a Johnsonian fiqure; his appearance is well rendered by the portrait at Fisher House by George Belcher but perhaps this fails to convey his ebullient vitality (plate 22). Soon an opportunity arose which gave scope to his gifts. In 1924 the freehold of a public house in Guildhall Street called the *Black Swan* came up for sale and it was acquired by C.U.C.A. for £10,000; a further £2,500 was required for repairs and alterations, and nearly all the money had to be borrowed. It was an enormous sum for those days and there were only one hundred and thirty Catholics in the university so that it was a great act of faith on the part of the few Catholic dons in residence who had to find the money. The purchase would probably not have been made without the relentless enthusiasm of one of them, Edward Bullough, Fellow of Caius and University Lecturer in Italian. Bullough had been received into the Catholic Church the previous year and had all the ardour of a neophyte. He was to enrich Cambridge Catholicism in more ways than one, since he left his house in Buckingham Road to the Friars Preachers at his death, which occured in 1934; this made possible the return of the Dominicans to Cambridge by the foundation of St Michael's Priory in 1938, exactly four hundred years after the extinction of the first Blackfriars. In 1924 Bullough was Treasurer of C.U.C.A. and it was his capacity for business and organisation which brought the project for buying the *Black Swan* to a successful conclusion. Fortunately Bishop Cary-Elwes of Northampton was also very much in favour and guaranteed the amount which was needed to bring the loan to the required sum.[13]

The *Black Swan* was well suited for the purpose of a chaplaincy. It was right in the centre of Cambridge and it was composed of an interesting and adaptable cluster of buildings[14] (plates 23, 24). The nucleus was made up of two old houses, originally separate and at right angles to each other, characteristic of the unpretentious but picturesque vernacular architecture of the town of which so few examples now survive. The house on the street, with its

22. *Fisher House: portrait of John Lopes. John Lopes, priest of the diocese of Birmingham, was Catholic chaplain at Cambridge 1922–8. He contributed greatly to the adaptation of the* Black Swan Inn, *which was bought in 1924 to become the chaplaincy for Catholics at the university. Portrait by George Belcher at Fisher House.* (Photograph by Eaden Lilley & Co.)

overhanging first storey, dates from the sixteenth century; the other house, reached by an alleyway, is probably early seventeenth century, though the cellars show signs of earlier, possibly medieval, work. At an unknown date they were joined. The public bar occupied the street front and became the present Oak Room and hall; the chaplain's dining room was originally the saloon bar.

127

Upstairs is a large room, known variously as the Great Room, the Great Chamber and the Chaplain's Study; it has oak beams, three south-facing windows admitting in abundance the clear East Anglian light, and fine proportions, so that it is one of the most pleasant rooms in Cambridge. In the nineteenth century two ranges were built, running south from the old house, to provide assembly rooms and a billiard room; they enclosed a pleasant courtyard.

23. *Fisher House and Guildhall Street. This sixteenth century house with overhanging first storey was the* Black Swan Inn, *which was named* Fisher House *in 1924 when it became the chaplaincy. The public bar occupied the ground floor along the street. Beyond the front of the old house is the nineteenth century building put up to house public rooms.* (Photograph by Alan Rooke)

128

24. Fisher House: view from the City Library. Southern front of the seventeenth century house built at right angles to the older house in Guildhall Street. The change in the roof line beyond the fourth dormer window (counting from the right) indicates the size of the original house which was later joined to the house in Guildhall Street whose southern gable can be seen on the left of the photograph. The three Georgian windows on the first floor are the windows of the Great Chamber. (Photograph by Andrew Gough)

It was decided to name the new chaplaincy *Fisher House* and a Birmingham architect, J. Arnold Crust, was commissioned to carry out the necessary alterations; the builders were a Cambridge firm, Sindall & Co. The house also bears the imprint of Fr Lopes's

129

generosity and taste; the tenement at Deritend was stripped of its splendour so that the panelling could be adapted to the dining room and the Oak Room;[15] the bottle-green leaded panes were inserted into the ground floor windows. One of the meeting rooms on the upper floor of the range further from the street became the chapel and Fr Lopes provided it with a baldachino, supported by plaster doric pillars (plate 25). The reredos to the altar was *lincrusta* in a green and gold damask design; this had been the frontal of the altar in Fr Nolan's day and he recognised it with delight when he came back, now Mgr Canon Nolan, Rector of St Mary Moorfields, to sing the Mass of St John Fisher on 4 May 1925 for the official opening of Fisher House.[16] C.U.C.A. found it difficult to finance the new development but in 1926 it was fortunate to receive £5,000 from the trustees of the estate of Percy Fitzgerald, a Catholic man of letters who had died the previous year. The gift was such a relief that it called for an outstanding commemoration and a tablet was put up in the chapel, carved by Eric Gill with an inscription composed by Ronald Knox. It is one of the treasures of Fisher House.[17]

Fr Lopes's chaplaincy was marked by special efforts on two fronts, the liturgical and the intellectual. He considered that the Catholic chaplaincy had inherited the spiritual obligations of the pre-Reformation foundations. Whereas previously mass and the divine office had been celebrated daily in college chapels, often for the souls of deceased benefactors, now only Fisher House could fulfil this duty. So Fr Lopes started a *Missa Cantata,* accompanied by Gregorian chant, which was celebrated on all Sundays and major feast days in full term. He also recited vespers in the chapel every week-day evening with his man-servant and *familiaris,* Edward Holmes, who was a Dominican Tertiary and wore the habit for this daily ceremony. Fr Lopes considered that the M.A. hood, worn above the surplice, was the correct choir dress for a secular priest but instead of wearing the hood trailing half way down the back, as is the current use, he enveloped the neck and shoulders with it like a short cape so that the long pointed hood, characteristic of English academic dress, could really be brought over the head like a monastic hood.

On the intellectual side Fr Lopes inaugurated the Dominican

25. Fisher House: the Old Upper Chapel. The baldachino, altars and screen (behind which was the sacristy) were made under the direction of Fr Lopes when the nineteenth century meeting room was adapted to form a chapel for Fisher House. It was opened on 4 May 1925. The reredos had previously been the frontal of the altar when the chaplaincy was in rented premises in Green Street.

This photograph shows the chapel prepared for Cardinal Bourne's visit on 4 May 1928, hence the prie-dieu and cushion before the altar; on the floor laurel and bay leaves are scattered, a characteristically Lopesian touch. (Reproduced from a contemporary postcard—Archives Fisher House)

lectures; this was the period of the neo-scholastic revival of which Jacques Maritain was the exponent best known in England, so that it was natural to turn to the Friars Preachers for lecturers to challenge the easy-going secular assumptions of Cambridge

131

youth. The Dominican lectures began in the Lent Term of 1926 and for several years Fr Hugh Pope came to give them with another Dominican, each lecturing on alternate evenings, originally in one of the conference rooms at the Guildhall and latterly in the university lecture rooms at Mill Lane. Fr Lopes considered that it was time that Catholics came to realise that they had a lot to give to the intellectual life of Cambridge; there was no inferiority complex about his Catholicism but a kind of welcoming confidence, something that he inherited perhaps from his Anglican past. Fr Lopes was confident but he was never aggressive; when G. G. Coulton, an erudite historian antagonistic to the Church, attended the lectures and questioned the lecturer provocatively afterwards, the chaplain invited him to cross the road to Fisher House and talk to the friars informally, and he came.[18] One example of the impact of the Lopesian chaplaincy is provided by the story of Oscar Morland, of Quaker stock, who came up to King's in 1922. He was persuaded by a friend to attend the first series of Dominican lectures in 1926 and, although he had no intention of becoming a Catholic, he was so impressed that he began a course of instruction with Fr Lopes and was received by him. Morland went on to a long and distinguished career in the Foreign Office.[19] There were others like him.

Fr Lopes was ahead of his time as an ecumenist; he never severed the friendships made when he had been an Anglican and the Church Unity Octave was observed at Fisher House long before it was popular among English Catholics. Another aspect of his chaplaincy was the constant concern for social questions and his care for the poor, especially through participation in annual missions to fruit pickers in the fens. During the General Strike of 1926 he was dismayed to hear of undergraduates volunteering as strike breakers and uttered the warning: 'If there is ever a class war in this country the universities of Oxford and Cambridge began it in 1926.'[20]

There was one grave drawback about Fr Lopes's style of chaplaincy: it was expensive. C.U.C.A., still burdened by debt, could not provide an income for the house and Fr Lopes, having run through two private fortunes, had no money left; this was the main reason for his leaving Cambridge in the summer of 1928 to become parish priest of Eynsham in Oxfordshire, where he remained until his death in 1961. He had set his mark on Fisher House and on the style of the university chaplaincy during the six years of his tenure; it is fair to say that, during the following decades, Fisher House continued to operate along the lines drawn by Fr Lopes, whatever the individual characteristics of the chaplains.

Fr George John MacGillivray was chosen to succeed Fr Lopes; for the first time the chaplain was a Cambridge graduate. Fr MacGillivray was a learned man, the son of an Edinburgh lawyer and brought up in the Episcopalian Church; he had studied at Edinburgh and Freiburg-im-Breisgau before coming up to Trinity in 1896 to read theology. His ministry in the Anglican Church took an unusual turn in 1910 when he volunteered for the Archbishop of Canterbury's mission to the Nestorian Christians in eastern Turkey.[21] While there his religious beliefs developed and he became convinced of the necessity of a visible centre of Christian unity; eventually he was received into the Catholic Church at Downside in 1919 and was ordained in 1922. He was fifty-two when he came to Cambridge.

Fr MacGillivray wrote of his conversion: 'I never had any emotional attraction to the Catholic Church. I never *wanted* to be a Catholic. I rather disliked the idea of it. I became a Catholic simply because I had to. It had become perfectly clear to me that the Catholic Church was the one true Church of God, and therefore I must belong to it.'[22] This sense of duty, unrelieved by any emotional appeal, was characteristic of Fr MacGillivray. After Fr Lopes, his chaplaincy lacked *brio* but it was undoubtedly serious. He instructed and received many converts and there were vocations to the priesthood.

Perhaps unfortunately, Fr MacGillivray was drawn into controversy with Anglicans. Vernon Johnson, a prominent Anglo-Catholic, had joined the Catholic Church in 1929 and published in the same year an account of his rejection of Anglicanism called *One Lord One Faith* (London, 1929). It was a little early to rush into print and it provoked a rejoinder, *One God and Father of all: A Reply to Father Vernon* (London, 1929), from Eric Milner-White, Dean of King's, and Wilfred Knox, Warden of the Cambridge house of the Oratory of the Good Shepherd, the brother of Ronald Knox. The argument of this book was that there are three great Christian communions, Rome, Constantinople and Canterbury; they all offer differing and beautiful interpretations of the historic faith, but it is unutterably wicked to transfer from one communion to another. Fr MacGillivray was not slow to point out, in *Father Vernon and his Critics* (London, 1930), that either proposition might be defended, but their combination is contradictory.

Fr MacGillivray's time as chaplain lasted four years but the economic crisis continued unabated and in 1932 he resigned 'for financial reasons'[23] and became parish priest of Maidstone. He was succeeded by Fr Alfred Newman Gilbey, a priest of the diocese of Brentwood, who had been an undergraduate at Trinity (1920–4) and President of the Fisher Society; he thus came to Cambridge with the great advantage of knowing the life of the Catholic academic community from the inside. To this was added the advantage of independent means, which allowed him to subsidise the work of Fisher House and thus to make it economically viable. Fr Gilbey's tenure of the chaplaincy was to last exactly one hundred terms, until Christmas 1965.

In the long history of Catholicism in Cambridge, we have now reached a period many of whose protagonists are still alive, so that a balanced judgment on persons and events is impossible. It would be premature, at so short a distance, to attempt to assess the relative importance of this decision or that development, to try to put into perspective what is new in relation to what is unchanging. Other chroniclers will have to be found for the setting up of the chaplaincy for women at Lady Margaret House in 1937, for the amalgamation of the two chaplaincies in 1966, for the saving of Fisher House from the wholesale demolition of the oldest quarter of Cambridge which preceded the development of Petty Cury in the nineteen-sixties, and for the reception of the ideas of the Second Vatican Council into the parishes and the chaplaincy.

There is, however, a consideration which should be always present to the minds of would-be Church historians. When surveying the life of the Christian community, so far as it can be discovered from the records of the past, it is dangerously easy to highlight one or other individual, to put forward current fashion as the equivalent of Christianity itself and to judge the achievements of the Church by the success or failure of a particular movement within it, be it in the area of theology, spirituality or ecclesiastical institutions. Such an approach easily turns to cynicism, the besetting sin of the historian, because movements lose their impetus and set up counter-trends; after surveying centuries of controversy, confusion and strife, it is easy to conclude that nothing has been achieved and to remain at the level of gentle irony at the ridiculous antics of religious men and women. And yet, in every age, the Kingdom of God grows because individuals become aware of the claims of the Gospel and progress in holiness through their union with the Lord Jesus who inhabits his community. This constant process can often pass unnoticed and, indeed, its consummation must remain ever hidden to all but the eyes of faith; but it is the essence of the life of the Church. The author of the Acts of the Apostles draws our attention to this by ending his account of the Church in his time, not with the martyrdom of an individual, however remarkable, nor with the triumph of a new movement, however radical, but with the picture of St Paul in Rome: 'He lived there two whole years at his own expense, and welcomed all who came to him, preaching the kingdom of God and teaching about the Lord Jesus Christ.'[24]

We would like to end our long story of Catholicism in Cambridge with a similar scene; in 1979 Mgr Gilbey celebrated the fiftieth anniversary of his ordination to the priesthood and a great gathering of graduates who had been at Cambridge during his chaplaincy attended the mass at Fisher House. One of these, Sir John Pilcher, who had been at Clare College from 1931 to 1934, wrote this account of his memories of a chaplain at work:

> I should like to record my view of the great civilising effect of Alfred's mission at Cambridge. When up at Cambridge I viewed it from a distance, since my contact with him was through friends and not direct. He was for many their first contact with the civilised man — *le vrai gentilhomme qui ne se pique de rien*. His influence was vast. As a priest he took the problems of each of his undergraduates with extreme seriousness. A good tutor should, of course, do this, but

scarcely with the dedication of a priest. Later I observed the range of 'pupils' he inspired. The rough were more numerous than the smooth. The Great Room pullulated with the earnest and the flippant, the young lovers and the idle (the latter were incarcerated upstairs until they had finished that essential essay, which they would otherwise never have completed). All came to love the lightly worn erudition, the Spanish *gravitas* and the elegance of manner, not to mention the humanity and the sense of humour. An almost unique combination of qualities and all subservient to the holiness of the priest. We glimpsed all that again during his Mass....[25]

Notes and References to Chapter 7

1. Our main sources in this chapter have been P. S. Wilkins, *Our Lady and the English Martyrs Cambridge* (Cambridge, 1955); *The Diocese of Northampton Centenary Souvenir 1850–1950* (London, Hoxton and Walsh [1950]); Garrett Sweeney, 'St Edmund's House; an embodiment' in *Bishops and Writers,* edited by Adrian Hastings (Wheathampstead, 1977), pp. 235–54; Garrett Sweeney, *St Edmund's House Cambridge: the First Eighty Years* (Cambridge, 1980); H. O. Evennett, 'The Cambridge Prelude to 1895: The Story of the Removal of the Ban on the Universities told from the Cambridge Angle', *The Dublin Review,* no. 437 (April, 1946), pp. 107–26. The story of Fisher House is told in [H. O. Evennett], *Fisher House Cambridge* (Cambridge, 1958) and in the published annual reports of C.U.C.A., starting in 1924. We have also used material first published in the *Fisher House Newsletter* (1979–81) and in a series of articles by M. N. L. Couve de Murville 'Fisher House: History and Pre-history' in *Forum* (a review published by students at Fisher House), nos. 1–4 [no date; *vere* 1980–1].
2. Text in *The Letters and Diaries of John Henry Newman* (Oxford, 1973), xxiii, p. 301, n. 1.
3. For instance, Sir John Simeon, who had asked Newman whether he should send his son to Oxford, wrote on 9 January 1868: 'I am getting very hopeless as to the Catholic future of England. All that can be done to spoil a great and noble future is in my poor opinion being done.' *Ibidem,* p. 382, n. 1.
4. It became the Oxford and Cambridge Catholic Education Board in 1937.
5. H. O. Evennett, 'The Cambridge Prelude to 1895', *The Dublin Review,* no. 437 (1946), p. 111.
6. G. Sweeney, *St Edmund's House, Cambridge,* p. 10.
7. *Ibidem,* p. 4 and Dom David Knowles's study, 'Edward Cuthbert Butler: 1858–1934', reprinted in *The Historian and Character* (Cambridge, 1963), pp. 299–303.
8. A. C. Benson, *Hugh: Memoirs of a Brother* (London, 1915), p. 141.
9. Quoted without ascription in Michael Hollings, 'Chaplaincraft 1963', *Clergy Review* 40 (1964) p. 5.
10. *Ibidem,* p. 5.
11. *C.U.C.A. Annual Report 1961,* p. 11.
12. The Baronetcy came in 1805 and in 1938 the fourth baronet was created Baron Roborough. The Barony of Ludlow was conferred on a younger branch of the family in 1897 and became extinct in 1922.

13. The other guarantors of the loan were Baron Anatole von Hügel; Dr Rastall, Fellow of Christ's and President of C.U.C.A.; E. Bullough; J. M. de Navarro, Fellow of Trinity; R. S. Momber and H. C. Norman. See *C.U.C.A. Annual Report 1924–1925*, p. 20.
14. See *City of Cambridge*, Royal Commission on Historical Monuments, 1959, ii, p. 330.
15. This gift is recorded by a small brass plaque in the Oak Room which reads: 'This panelling was presented to the Association in 1924 by Fr John Lopes University Chaplain 1922–1928.'
16. The reredos was in use until the old chapel was pulled down in 1975 to make way for the present Assembly Hall; it is now fixed to the wall in the staircase next to the Assembly Hall.
17. Unfortunately after the rebuilding of 1975 the tablet was relegated to an obscure and indeed vulnerable position in the entrance to the Assembly Hall.
18. Cf. Professor W. L. Edge, 'Reminiscences', *Fisher House Newsletter 1981*, p. 25.
19. Sir Oscar Morland, G.B.E., K.C.M.G., was Ambassador to Indonesia 1953–6, Assistant Under-secretary at the Foreign Office 1956–9, and Ambassador to Japan from 1959 until his retirement in 1963. He died on 20 May 1980.
20. Quoted by W. L. Edge, 'Reminiscences', *Fisher House Newsletter 1981*, p. 26.
21. See the fascinating account of Fr MacGillivray's four years in the now vanished society of the 'Assyrian Christians' in his book, *Through the East to Rome* (London, 1931).
22. *Ibidem*, p. 249.
23. *C.U.C.A. Annual Report 1931–32*, p. 9.
24. Acts of the Apostles 28: 30–1.
25. Quoted in *Fisher House Newsletter 1979*, p. 14.

Appendix I

Provisional list of members of the University of Cambridge who were executed or who died in prison for the Catholic Faith during the period of the Reformation, arranged chronologically.

(This material was kindly collected for publication in *Catholic Cambridge* by Mr P. C. Barry, Research Assistant for the cause of the English and Welsh Martyrs at the Office of Vice-Postulation, Farm Street.)

Name and status	College	References to Cambridge connections. (All references to Venn, *Al.Can.* in this Appendix are to Part I.) Manner and place of death.
John HOUGHTON, St priest Carthusian monk	?	Ven, *Al.Can.,* ii, p. 413; B.A., Ll.B. and B.D. of Cambridge acc. to Cooper, i, p. 52, but degrees not recorded. *ROE,* iii, p. 225 agrees; no refs. Executed, Tyburn, 1535.
Richard REYNOLDS, St priest Bridgettine monk	Corpus Christi	Venn, *Al.Can.,* iii, p. 445; B.A. 1505–6, M.A. 1508–9, B.D. 1512–13. Fellow of Corpus Christi, 1510. University preacher, 1509. *ROE,* iii, p. 214 agrees; no refs. Executed, Tyburn, 1535.
John HAILE, Bl priest	King's Hall	*LP* viii, no. 615: letter of Master of King's Hall to Thos. Cromwell, 30 April, 1535. See also *LEM,* i, p. 17, n. Executed, Tyburn, 1535.
William EXMEW, Bl priest Carthusian monk	Christ's	Ven, *Al.Can.,* ii, p. 113 *ROE,* iii, p. 226: 'a Cambridge man of exceptional ability'; no refs. Executed, Tyburn, 1535.
Sebastian NEWDIGATE, St priest Carthusian monk	?	Van Ortroy, p. 53, citing Arundel MSS in BL. See L. Whatmore, *Clergy Review* (July 1946), p. 356. Executed Tyburn, 1535.

John FISHER, St Bishop of Rochester Cardinal	Michael- house etc.	*BRUC,* pp. 229–30. Admitted scholar of Michaelhouse c. 1483; Fellow c. 1491. Ordained priest 1491, to title of Fellowship. Master of Michaelhouse, 1496–8. M.A. 1491. D.Th. 1510. Senior Proctor, 1494–5. Vice-Chancellor, 1501. First Lady Margaret Reader in Divinity, 1502. Chancellor of the University, 1504; re-elected for life, 1514. President of Queens', 1505–8. Executed, Tower Hill, 1535.
John ROCHESTER, Bl priest Carthusian monk	?	Same references as for Blessed Sebastian Newdigate above. Executed, York, 1537.
Richard FETHERSTON, Bl or FETHERSTONHALGH	?	*BRUC,* p. 226. *BRUO,* p. 204. Admitted questionist at Cambridge, Michaelmas Term, 1499. B.A. Incorporated at Oxford by 1505. M.A. Oxford, 1505. Grace *ad eundem gradum* granted at Cambridge, 1506–7. Fellow of University College, Oxford and Queen's College, Oxford. Executed, Smithfield, 1540.
German GARDINER, Bl layman	Prob. Trinity Hall	Venn, *Al.Can.,* ii, p. 192; prob. of Trinity Hall. Cooper, i, p. 83: 'educated in this university, probably in Trinity Hall'. Executed, Tyburn, 1544.
Everard HANSE, Bl priest	?	Challoner, p. 13: 'performed his higher studies in the University of Cambridge.' (MS life). *LEM,* ii, p. 250: 'sent to Cambridge', ref. to MS life in AAW, ii, p. 175, used by Challoner. Anstruther, i, p. 145: according to the MS life, he studied at Cambridge and was promoted to a fat living. 'He cannot be traced at Cambridge, nor has anyone of that name been discovered holding a living.' Executed, Tyburn, 1581.
John NUTTER, Bl priest	St John's	Venn, *Al.Can.,* iii, p. 272: matric. sizar from St John's, 1573. Executed, Tyburn, 1584.

Richard GWYN, St alias WHITE layman	St John's	T. Dempsey, *Richard Gwyn* (Farnworth, 1970) p. 13. Went for a short time to Oxford; admitted Dowman sizar for Dr Bullock, Master of St John's College, Cambridge, on 20 March 1559. Cooper, i, p. 494, and Venn, *Al.Can.,* iv, p. 388 confuse him with another Richard White, matric. from Christ's in 1571. Executed, Wrexham, 1584.
Thomas ALFIELD, Bl priest	King's	Venn, *Al.Can.,* i, p. 15; Matric. 1568, B.A. 1572–3. Fellow of King's 1571–5. Executed, Tyburn, 1585.
John FINGLEY or FINGLOW, Ven. priest	Caius	Venn, *Al.Can.,* ii, p. 140: Matric. sizar from Caius, 1573. Butler *(promus)* at Caius for three or four years. Forced to leave by anti-Catholic feeling, apparently without a degree. Executed, York, 1586.
William DEAN, Bl priest	Magdalene & Caius	Venn, *Al.Can.,* ii, p. 16: Matric. sizar from Magdalene, 1575. Adm. pensioner at Caius, 1577, aged 20. Executed, Mile End Green, 1588.
Ralph CROCKETT, Bl priest	Christ's	Venn, *Al.Can.,* i, p. 420: Matric. sizar from Christ's, 1568. Anstruther, i, p. 93: about three years in Cambridge; later went to Gloucester Hall, Oxford, for a year. Executed, Chichester, 1588.
John HEWETT alias WELDON, Bl priest	Caius	Described in a contemporary hostile pamphlet, dated 24 October 1588, as 'sometime student in Caius Colledge in Cambridge'. Copies at Lambeth Palace and Oscott College; reprinted in *Harleian Miscell.* 10, pp. 380 seqq. and in *CRS* 32 (1932), pp. 410–28, (quotation above on p. 414). Venn, *Gonv. and Caius,* i, p. 106: 'He appears to have been at our college, but his name is not in the records.' Executed, Mile End Green, 1588.

CATHOLIC CAMBRIDGE

Montford SCOTT, Ven. priest	Trinity Hall	Venn, *Al.Can.,* iv, p. 32: Munford Scott, Matric. sizar from Trinity Hall, 1565; scholar, 1566. Anstruther, i, p. 303: captured in Cambridge 5 June 1578, having come into England on 19 June 1577 after studies in Douai and ordination at Brussels. Executed, Fleet Street, 1591.
Thomas PORMORT, Ven. priest	Trinity	Venn, *Al.Can.,* iii, p. 381: Matric. Trinity College, 1575. No record of a degree. Executed, St Paul's Churchyard, 1592.
Thomas MEETHAM, priest Jesuit	Trinity	Venn, *Al.Can.,* iii, p. 180: Matric. Trinity College, 1551. B.A. 1554–5, M.A. 1558, Fellow 1555. H. Foley, *Records of the English Province of the Society of Jesus,* ii, p. 608. Died in Wisbech Castle after seventeen years' imprisonment, 1592.
Henry WALPOLE, St priest Jesuit	Peterhouse	Venn, *Al.Can.,* iv. p. 324: Admitted pensioner at Peterhouse, 1575. Matric. 1575 Executed, York, 1595.
Philip HOWARD, St Earl of Arundel layman	St John's	Venn, *Al.Can.,* ii, p. 416: M.A. 1576, St John's. Died in Tower of London after ten years' imprisonment, 1595.
William ANDLEBY, Bl priest	St John's	Venn, *Al.Can.,* i, p 33: Matric. pensioner from St John's, 1567, B.A., 1571–2. Executed, York, 1597.
William (Maurus) SCOTT, Bl priest Benedictine	Trinity & Trinity Hall	Venn, *Al.Can.,* iv, p. 33: Matric. sizar from Trinity College, Lent 1593–4; Ll.B. from Trinity Hall, 1600. Camm. *N.M. Monks,* pp. 189–91, migrated to Trinity Hall in 1596. Executed, Tyburn, 1612.

James (Laurence) MABBS priest Benedictine	Emmanuel	Venn, *Al.Can.*, iii, p. 123: James Mabbs, admitted sizar at Emmanuel, 1612. Matric. 1612.B.A. 1615–6. *Third Douai Diary*, CRS 10 (1911), pp. 136, 143. H. N. Birt, *Obit Book of the English Benedictines* (Edinburgh, 1913), p. 22. Died in Newgate Prison in chains, 1641.
Bartholomew (Alban) ROE, St priest Benedictine	?	Challoner, p. 407: 'sent to the university of Cambridge.' No other evidence; not mentioned in Venn. Executed, Tyburn, 1642.
Hugh GREEN, Bl priest	Peterhouse	Venn, *Al.Can.*, ii, p. 255: Matric. sizar from Peterhouse, c. 1601. Scholar, 1603. B.A. 1605–6. M.A. 1609. Anstruther, ii, p. 137. Executed, Dorchester, 1642.
John GOODMAN, Ven. priest	St John's	Venn, *Al.Can.*, ii, p. 236: Matric. sizar from St John's, 1612; B.A. 1616–17. Anstruther, ii, p. 132. Died in Newgate Prison, 1642 or 1645.
Henry HEATH, Ven. priest O.F.M.	Corpus Christi	Venn, *Al.Can.*, ii, p. 347: Matric. sizar from Corpus Christi 1617; B.A. 1620–1. No M.A. recorded. Executed, Tyburn, 1643.
Henry MORSE, St priest Jesuit	Corpus Christi	Venn, *Al.Can.*, iii, p. 216: Admitted Corpus Christi, 1612. Executed, Tyburn, 1645.
Edward COLEMAN, Bl layman	Trinity	Venn, *Al.Can.*, i, p. 369: Admitted pensioner at Trinity, 1651. Matric. 1651. B.A. 1655–6; M.A. 1659. Executed, Tyburn, 1678.
Anthony TURNER, Bl priest Jesuit	Peterhouse St John's	Venn, *Al.Can.* iv, p. 273: Admitted sizar at Peterhouse, 1644. Migrated to St John's, 1645, aged 17. Matric. 1645. B.A. 1647–8. Executed, Tyburn, 1679.
William HOWARD, Bl Viscount Stafford layman	St John's	Venn, *Al.Can.*, ii, p. 417: Matric. fellow-commoner from St John's, 1624. Executed, Tower Hill, 1680.

143

Edward TURNER priest Jesuit	St John's & Corpus Christi	Venn, *Al.Can.*, iv, p. 274: Admitted pensioner at St John's. 1642. Matric. 1646. B.A., 1646–7. M.A. from Corpus Christi, 1662. Incorporated at Oxford, 1663. Brother of Anthony Turner, S.J. Died in the Gatehouse Prison, 1681.

Appendix II

Missionary Rectors and Parish Priests of Our Lady and the English Martyrs, Cambridge.

Canon Thomas Quinlivan	1843–1883
Mgr Provost Christopher Scott	1883–1922
Canon James Bernard Marshall	1922–1946
Canon Edmund Stokes	1947–1961
Mgr Canon Frank Diamond	1961–1968
Canon Paul Taylor	1968–1980
Father Anthony Philpot	1980–

Appendix III

Catholic Chaplains at the University of Cambridge.

Edmund Nolan	1896–1902
Arthur Stapylton Barnes	1902–1916
James Bernard Marshall	1918–1922
John Ludlow Lopes	1922–1928
George John MacGillivray	1928–1932
Alfred Newman Gilbey	1932–1965
Richard Laurence Incledon	1966–1977
Maurice Noël Léon Couve de Murville	1977–1982
David Christopher Jenkins, O.S.B.	1982–

Index

Acton, Cardinal Charles, 100
Alabaster, William, 80
Alcock, John, 56, 58
Aldrich, Robert, 66
Alford, John, 107–8
All Saints', Fulbourn, 46
All Saints' by the Castle, 5
All Saints' in Jewry, 5, 37
Andrewes, Lancelot, 81
Apreece, Ven. Robert, 82
Ashton, Hugh, 59
Audley, Lord, 71
Augustinian canons, 5–6, 70
Austin friars, 30–34, 43, 44, 68

Baker, Philip, 73
Banks, Christopher, 84
Bargrave, John, 84
Barnes, Arthur Stapylton, 123–4
Barnes, Robert, 68–9
Barnwell Priory, 6, 10, 18, 68, 69,
 70
Bassett, Joshua, 87
Bateman, William, 38–40
Beaufort, Lady Margaret, 58, 59,
 60n, 116
Becket, St Thomas, 13, 14
Benedictines, 78, 79, 87, 122
Benet House, 122–3
Benson, A. C., 123
Benson, R. H., 123
Bilney, Thomas, 68
Bisshop, Geoffrey, 46
Bolt, Clement, 88
Boniface IX, Pope, 18
Botolph, St, 2
Bourne, Cardinal Francis, 124
Bridgett, T. E., 108–9
Bridgettines, 56, 66–7, 69
Bucer, Martin, 74
Buckingham College, 71
Bullock, George, 73
Bullough, Edward, 126
Bury St Edmunds, 87, 92
Butler, Cuthbert, 122
Butler, William, 80

Caius, John, 73, 76, 77
Cambridge (town), ii (map), xii
 (illus.), 1–12, 55, 87, 100, 103–4,
 105
Cambridge, University of, *passim*
 admission of RCs to, 87, 100,
  104, 120–1
 Boat Club, 101, 110–11n
 Catholic Association, 121, 123,
  125, 126, 130, 132
 Catholic Chaplaincy, 71, 121,
  122, 123–36
 independence, 17–19
 Library, 41–3, 66, 70
 origins, 13–16
 seals, 15 (illus.)
 studies, 19–22, 34, 35, 41–3, 71
 theology, 20–2, 27–8, 64
Cambridge Camden Society, 106,
 107
Cambridge Castle, 4, 5, 90
Carawey, John, 44–8
Carmelites, 10, 23, 28–30, 33–4, 43,
 47, 86, 92, 120
Carthusians, 56, 67, 69
Cartwright, Humphrey, 76–7
Cartwright, Thomas, 77
Cary-Elwes, Bishop, 126
Catholic Emancipation, 99
Ceollach, Bishop, 2
Champion, John, 93, 94
Charles I, King, 79, 81
Charles II, King, 86
Cheke, John, 64
Chesterton, 5, 11, 28, 83–4, 118,
 120
Cheveley Hall, 86, 88, 92
Christ's College, 58–9, 67, 73, 75,
 76, 77, 80, 100, 104
Christopherson, John, 74
Clare College, 11, 37, 46, 68, 77,
 80, 81, 135
Clerk, John, 66
Cole, Henry, 74
Cole, William, 93–4
Coleman, Bl. Edward, 84, 86

'College of the Holy Apostles', 82, 85, 87, 91, 93, 94
Compton, Philip, 85
Corpus Christi College, 7n, 8, 10, 38, 39 (illus.), 40–1, 44, 62, 67, 69, 70, 75, 76, 77, 79
Coulton, G. G., 132
Cosin, Edmund, 73
Cosin, John, 81, 86
Cranmer, Thomas, ix, 68, 72
Crashaw, Richard, 81, 82, 84
Cromwell, Oliver, ix, 85, 88

de Balsham, Hugh, 36
de Clare, Lady Elizabeth, 37
de Coventry, Vincent, 25
de Hornby, John, 29
de Letheringset, John, 27
de Lisle, Thomas, 32
de Nekton, Humphrey, 28
de Stanton, Hervey, 37
de Swaffham, Nicholas, 47–8
de Valence, Countess, 37–8
de Vere, Lady Alice, 26
de Walcote, William, 30
Digby, Kenelm Henry, 101–3
Diuma, Bishop, 2
Doket, Andrew, 44–5, 50
Dominicans, 10, 23, 26–8, 33–4, 43, 44, 69, 73, 85, 94, 126, 130–2
Douai, 79, 85, 102
Dover, Earl of, 86
Downing College, 123
Dowsing, William, 83–4
Dryden, John, 87
Dunwich, John, 28

Edward I, King, 5, 10, 17n, 30
Edward II, King, 18, 36–7
Edward VI, King, 66, 71
Elizabeth I, Queen, 66, 70, 73, 74, 75, 76, 77, 78, 80, 83
Ely, abbey, 3, 4, 6, 69, 70
   bishops of, 4, 14, 16, 17, 18, 19, 32, 36, 56, 64, 70, 83, 87, 95
Emmanuel College, 26, 76, 80
English College, Rome, 84, 103, 108, 113
Erasmus, 59–60, 65, 66, 67, 68
Ethelreda, St, 3, 70
Eugenius IV, Pope, 18

Eustace, Henry, 8, 10
Eustace, J. Chetwode, 100
Exmew, Bl. William, 67, 69
Eyre family, 100

Fagius, Paul, 74
Felix, St, 2, 3
Ferrar, Nicholas, 81–2
Fetherston, Bl. Richard, 69
Fisher, St John, 11, 54 (illus.), 55n, 58, 59, 60n, 61 (illus.), 64, 66, 67, 69, 77, 116, 119 (illus.)
Fisher House, 126–30 (illus.), 132, 133, 134
Fisher Society, 123, 124, 134, 135
Fitzgerald, Percy, 130
Flete, William, 32
Fleury, John, 98
Flower, Benjamin, 99
Foxe, Richard, 59, 62, 65, 66
Francis, Alban, 87
Franciscans, 23–5, 33–4, 43, 56, 69
Fraternity of the Holy Sepulchre, 6
Friars of the Sack, 6

Gardiner, Bl. German, 20
Gardiner, Stephen, 64, 66, 72
Gerard, John, 91
Gilbertian canons, 5
Gilbey, Alfred Newman, 134, 135–6
Gill, Eric, 130
God's House, 11, 59
Gonville, Edmund, 38
Gonville and Caius College, 73, 75, 76, 77–8, 87, 88, 126
Gonville Hall, 38, 69, 73
Goodrich, Thomas, 70
Great St Mary's, 8, 10, 34, 38, 41, 55, 56n, 57 (illus.), 58, 74, 76
Green, Bl. Hugh, 79
Greenwood, William, 94
Grim, John, 14
Guala, Cardinal, 5
Guild of Corpus Christi, 7n, 8
Guild of St Mary, 6, 8
Guild of the Annunciation, 8
Gwyn, St Richard, 78–9

Hackluit, Jeremiah, 85
Hacomblen, Robert, 62
Hanse, Bl. Everard, 78

Heath, Ven. Henry, 79
Heaton, John, 84
Henry III, King, 5, 16, 23, 26, 28
Henry VI, King, 65
Henry VII, King, 58, 59, 62, 116
Henry VIII, King, 37, 56, 64, 65,
    66, 69, 77, 83
Heskins, Thomas, 73, 77
Hinton, Walter, 67
Holmes, Edward, 130
Holtby, Richard, 78
Holy Trinity (church), 5, 77, 80, 83
Hooker, Richard, 84
Hopeman, Thomas, 29–30
Hornyold, Bishop, 95
Houghton, St John, 67, 69
Howard, St Philip, 78
Howard, Bl. William, 86
Hullier, John, 72
Huddleston, Sir Edmund, 79, 90–1
Huddleston, Edward, 103–4, 110
Huddleston, Ferdinand (d.1808), 93,
    94–5
Huddleston, Ferdinand (d.1890),
    99–100
Huddleston, Henry, 91
Huddleston, Colonel Henry, 91
Huddleston, Sir John, 90
Huddleston, John, OSB, 86
Huddleston, John, SJ, 85, 91, 93
Huddleston or Dormer, John, 91
Huddleston, Major Richard, 98, 99,
    100, 103, 104
Huddleston, Thomas, 95
Huddleston, William, OSB, 95–6,
    96–7n
Huddleston family, 90–6, 98–9, 105

Innocent VI, Pope, 37–8
Institute of the Blessed Virgin
    Mary, 120

James I, King, 56, 78, 80
James II, King, 86–8, 91
Jermyn family, 92
Jesuits, 77, 78, 79, 81, 82, 84, 85,
    87, 91, 92, 93, 94, 104, 108
Jesus College, 6, 56, 59
Jews, 5, 10, 24
John, King, 5, 13

John XXII, Pope, 17–18
Johnson, Vernon, 133–4

King's College, 55, 59, 62, 72, 73,
    74, 75, 77, 81, 118, 132
King's College Chapel, 11, 22, 28,
    37, 40, 60–4, 65 (illus.), 74, 101,
    102
King's Hall, 30, 36–7, 44, 56, 66,
    71, 73
Kirtling, 107–8
Knox, Ronald, 130
Knox, Wilfred, 133–4

Lady Margaret House, 134
Latimer, Hugh, ix, 64, 68–9, 71, 72
Laud, Archbishop William, 81, 84,
    86, 88
Legge, Dr, 78
Leyburn, Dr, 85
Little St Mary's, 4, 5, 36, 84, 108
Linton, 92, 98
Llandaff House, 123, 124
Lomax, John, 92
Lopes, John, 125–6, 127 (illus.),
    129–33
Lyne-Stephens, Mrs, 114, 116

MacGillivray, G. J., ix, 133–4, 138
Madingley Hall, 46n, 47 (illus.), 94
Magdalene College, 71, 100
Maldon, Thomas, 29
Manning, Cardinal H.E., 108, 118n,
    120
Margaret of Anjou, 44, 50n
Marshall, James Bernard, 124–5
Martin V, Pope, 18
Martin, John, 93
Martindale, C. C., 125
Marvell, Andrew, 82
Mary, Queen, 64, 66, 72, 76, 77, 90
Melton, William, 58
Michaelhouse, 37, 64, 67
Milner, John, 103, 104
Milner-White, Eric, 133–4
Milton, John, 80
Mitchell, Thomas, 93, 94
Moberly, Rev., 99
Montagu, Richard, 81
More, St Thomas, 59, 64, 67
Morland, Oscar, 132, 138n

Morris, John, 107–8
Morse, St Henry, 79
Morton, Thomas, 84
Mount Saint Bernard Abbey, 103, 107
Mountjoy, Lord, 59, 66, 69

Natures, Edmund, 68
Newdigate, Bl. Sebastian, 67, 69
Newman, Cardinal J. H., 106
Newton, Sir Isaac, 87
Nolan, Edmund, 121, 122, 123, 130
Norfolk, fifteenth Duke of, 114, 122
North, Lady Frederica, 109
North, first Lord, 70
North, eleventh Lord, 109–10
Nutter, Bl. John, 78

Offa, King of Mercia, 3
Old Schools, 41–3 (illus.), 46n
Ormanetto, Nicholas, 74
Our Lady and the English Martyrs (church), 112 (illus.), 114, 115 (illus.), 116, 117 (illus.), 118, 122
Our Lady Immaculate and St Philip Neri (church), 109
Oxford, University of, 13, 14, 16, 20, 25, 30, 31, 33, 55, 106, 121, 125
Oxford Movement, ix, 105–6

Paley, Frederick Apthorp, 107–8
Parker, Matthew, ix
Paris family, 92
Paul III, Pope, 69
Peada, King of Mercia, 2
Pemberton, Christopher, 98
Pembroke College, 37–8, 62, 73, 81
Pennington, William, 93
Penda, King of Mercia, 2
Perne, Andrew, 73
Persons, Robert, 77
Peterhouse, 36, 38, 79, 81, 84
Petre, George, 100
Petre, William, second Lord, 82
Petre, William, eleventh Lord, 100
Phillipps de Lisle, Ambrose, 102–3, 105, 106, 107, 108

Picheford, Sir Geoffrey, 30
Pico, Sheriff, 5
Pied Friars, 6
Pius V, Pope, 76
Pius IX, Pope, 110
Pius XI, Pope, 63
Pius XII, Pope, 63
Pole, Cardinal Reginald, 72, 73–6
Pope, Hugh, 132
Pugin, A. W., 105, 108

Queens' College, 11, 28, 40, 44, 45, 48n, 49 (illus.), 50n, 51 (illus.), 55, 58, 59, 66
Queen's College of St Margaret and St Bernard, 44–5, 46, 47, 50n
Quinlivan, Canon Thomas, 105, 107, 113, 118

Randolph, Berkeley William, 125
Ramsey (abbey), 4, 6
Rawlyn, Thomas, 68
Redington, Thomas, 104
Regent House, 41, 45 (illus.)
Reynolds, St Richard, 67, 69
Richard II, King, 11
Richard III, King, 35
Riddell, Bishop, 113, 116, 118n, 122
Ridley, Nicholas, ix, 72
Rigby, St John, 79
Robinson College, 35
Rochester, Bl. John, 67, 69
Roe, St Alban, 79
Roger of Wendover, 13–14
Round Church, 5, 6, 75, 83, 106
Rotherham, Thomas, 42, 43, 46n
Russell, Sir William, 88
Ruthall, Thomas, 59, 65

St Alban's School, 118, 120
St Andrew's Church, 103–5, 108–9, 113, 118
St Andrew's School, 118, 120
St Andrew the Less, 6, 104
St Bede's School, 120
St Benet's Church, 4, 8, 38, 39 (illus.), 40
St Botolph's Church, 38, 44
St Botolph's Church, Hadstock, 2–3, 4

St Catharine's College, 11, 38, 55, 73
St Clement's Church, 4, 10, 77, 109
St Edmund's College, Ware, 102–3, 121
St Edmund's House, 122, 123
St Edward's Church, 4, 65 (illus.), 68
St Giles's Church, 6, 109
St John's College, 6, 58–9, 61 (illus.), 70–1, 73, 75, 78, 84, 85, 107, 108
St John's Hospital, 6, 11, 36, 43, 58
St John Zachary's Church, 37
St Laurence's Church, 118
St Laurence's School, 120
St Mary's School, 120
St Michael's Church, 36, 95
St Michael's Priory, 126
St Omer, College of, 91
St Peter's Church, 5, 36
St Philip Howard's Church, 118
St Radegund's Priory, 6, 10, 56, 58
Sawston Hall, 79, 86, 90–6, 98, 100, 103, 105, 118
Sayer, Robert, 78
Scot, Cuthbert, 73, 75
Scott, Canon Christopher, 113–4, 116, 120, 122, 125
Scott, John, 104
Sergeant, John, 84
Shanley, Fr B., 104
Shelford, Robert, 81
Sidney Sussex College, 25, 76, 87
Simeon, Charles, ix, 96
Sisters of the Holy Family of Bordeaux, 120
Spencer, George, 103
Stokes, John, 29

Thomas of Eccleston, 23–4
Thomas of Strassburg, 30–1
Thorney (abbey), 4, 70
Throckmorton, Francis, 85
Traherne, Bartholomew, 69
Trinity College, 11, 25, 37, 56, 59, 70, 71, 73, 74, 75, 80, 82, 84, 87, 101, 102, 107, 125, 133, 134
Trinity Hall, 10, 38, 40, 64, 66, 68
Trussebut, John, 27
Tunstall, Cuthbert, 66
Turner, Bl. Anthony, 84, 86

Universities' Catholic Education Board, 121, 125

Vatican II, ix, 63, 134
Vaughan, Cardinal Herbert, 120–1, 122
von Hügel, Baron Anatole, 118, 120, 121, 122

Waldegrave, Lord, 92
Walpole, Christopher, 78
Walpole, St Henry, 78
Walpole, Horace, 100–101
Walsh, Bishop, 104
Wareing, William, 105, 108, 110
Watson, Thomas, 73–4
West, Nicholas, 64–5
Whitford, Richard, 66–7, 69
William III, King, 92
William the Conqueror, 4
Willoughby, Richard, 77
Wiseman, Cardinal Nicholas, 105
Woodville, Elizabeth, 44
Wyflete, William, 46

Young, John, 73.